WHAT OTH

Broken and Blue is masterfully crafted to help identify the brokenness of the human spirit. While everyone has a different level of sorrow, no one is exempt. Scott Silverii worked in the trenches of law enforcement and dodged the political landmines as chief of police. Yet, more importantly is the sage advice that he's illuminated using the Word of God.
—Jim McNeff, partner and managing editor, Law Enforcement Today, author, police commander (ret.)

* * *

Chief Scott Silverii nails it again! Combining real-life experience, raw emotions, and what it's really like out there on the bricks. This book is saving lives.
Sean Riley
President & Founder - Safe Call Now

* * *

Life will get to even the best of us. Scott Silverii's book *Broken and Blue: A Policeman's Guide to Health, Healing, and Hope* walks us to the pain and through the pain, into a place where understanding is fostered, forgiveness of ourselves and others begins, and freedom from the chains is found. This isn't just a good read, it is a work in progress.
Olivia Johnson, DM
Founder, Blue Wall Institute

* * *

Every first responder that calls themselves a son or daughter (or seeker) of God should read and respond to this book.

Scott has done something almost unheard of in our career fields: he's taken off the armor of the uniform and laid bare his struggles, as well as his successes, to give us a practical guide, in our language, to find the freedom that Jesus intended us to have.

I pray this will bless you as much as it did me!
Ryan Padgett
Chairman, Board of Directors
10-33 Foundation

* * *

"Deeply personal, educational, and at times...difficult to read without tears. All LEO families need this book."
Liliana Hart
New York Times bestselling author and LEO spouse of Blue Marriage founder.

* * *

Having served 21 years in law enforcement, which included commanding a triple homicide active shooter incident, I know police officers deserve the chance to heal from the wounds inflicted while serving others.

Chief Scott Silverii's Broken and Blue guides officers through the process of healing, while giving them hope for restored health.
David Oliver
Chief of Police (Retired)

BROKEN AND BLUE

A POLICEMAN'S GUIDE TO HEALTH, HOPE AND HEALING

CHIEF SCOTT SILVERII, PHD

CONTENTS

Foreword by Pastor Jimmy Evans   vii
Copyright   ix
Introduction   xi

1. Finding Freedom   1
2. Defining Personal Pain   6
3. Avoiding Past Pain   11
4. Managing Personal Pain   18
5. Our Past Reminds Us, Not Defines Us   25
6. Spiritual Freedom   30
7. Learning To Forgive   34
8. Remaining Spiritually Free   45
9. Inner Vows   52
10. Judgments   59
11. PTSD and Soul Scars   65
12. Unseen Enemies   77
13. Personal Baggage   88
14. Distorted Image of God   93
15. Distorted Self-Image   98
16. Wrong Relationships   105
17. Unhealthy Personalities   109
18. Anger and Hostility   114
19. Depression   122
20. Addiction   129
21. The Daily Walk Fortress   135
22. The Transformed Mind   140
23. Accountability   145
24. Boundaries   149
25. Consequences   154
26. Restoration   158
27. Renewal and the Fortress Against Spiritual Warfare   163
28. The Key to Freedom   168

Dr. Scott Silverii 173
Your Mission Assignment 175
Also by Chief Scott Silverii, PhD 177

Foreword by Pastor Jimmy Evans

Law enforcement officers and their families live in a world of hurt, and that pain is accumulated over years of on the job trauma. LEOs and their spouses suffer, usually in silence, as the pain manifests into addiction, depression, alcoholism, suicide, and PTSD, just to name a few.

When Scott asked me to write the foreword for this book, I was honored to do so, because during the course of decades of ministry and marriage counseling, I've seen what this pain can do to first responder marriages and families, and the destruction is very real.

There are few resources available to help those who walk the thin blue line. There are even fewer resources that show you how to heal with Christ walking beside you. Scott has lived the life, he's battled, and he's been healed by the grace of God. There's no one better to share with you and show you how God can turn your past pains into something incredible for His glory.

Law enforcement officers and first responders everywhere should read this book, whether still on the job or retired. It gives hope, it gives healing, and it'll change your life and the legacy of your family.

Jimmy Evans
Founder of MarriageToday

© 20218 *Scott Silverii*

All rights reserved. No part of this publication may be reproduced, distributed, or transmitted in any form or by any means, including photocopying, recording, or other electronic or mechanical methods, without the prior written permission of the publisher, except in the case of brief quotations embodied in critical reviews and certain other noncommercial uses permitted by copyright law. For permission requests, contact Five Stones Press or Dr. Scott Silverii

All Scripture quotations, unless otherwise indicated, are taken from the New American Standard Bible, ©1960, 1962, 1963, 1968, 1971, 1972, 1973, 1975, 1977, 1995 by The Lockman Foundation. Used by permission.

Other versions used are:

KJV—King James Version. Authorized King James Version.

NIV—Scripture taken from the Holy Bible, New International Version®. Copyright © 1973, 1978, 1984 by International Bible Society. Used by permission of Zondervan Publishing House. All rights reserved.

First Edition

Publisher: Five Stones Press, Dallas, Texas

contact@bluemarriage.com

For quantity sales, textbooks, and orders by trade bookstores or wholesalers contact Five Stones Press at publish@fivestonespress.net

Five Stones Press is owned and operated by Five Stones Church, a nonprofit 501c3 religious organization. Press name and logo are trademarked. Contact publisher for use.

Dr. Scott Silverii's website is scottsilverii.com

Printed in the United States of America

INTRODUCTION

Everyone was busting each other's balls about how jacked over we got in our divorce settlements. We laughed about how much child support we paid, as if it were a badge of honor. Our seventieth-floor drug task force office wasn't only where federal investigations were made, but it was also a part-time boys' club therapy session.

The guys who had been remarried once were plotting about their next divorce as I beat my chest over the new woman in my life. I hadn't seen my sweet four-year-old son in six months, but I was taking care of someone else's child as we played house. My ex-wife and I were locked in a vicious, emotion-driven battle over out-of-state custody, but there I was, comparing notes with the most important people in my life: my brothers in blue.

Maneuvering through New Orleans's cruddy streets after hours was already tough enough, but I swerved my undercover police unit over to the shoulder and slammed it into park. I couldn't breathe. I clutched my chest to force air into my lungs. The only thing I could hear was a crazy gasping sound that wheezed out of my mouth. I was dying, and I sure didn't want to crash my unit while doing so.

Introduction

Looking in the rearview mirror, I didn't even recognize the shattered, broken shell of a man who only a year earlier was teaching fourth grade Sunday school at the local church while my wife and toddler son enjoyed the nursery.

My eyes were full of water. Hot tears streamed down my face and into an overgrown beard. The arrogant bragging with the guys overwhelmed me until I couldn't think straight. It was a searing pain. I was a pathetic mess.

My cruiser rocked on old shocks as traffic zipped by. Horns honked and caring citizens offered encouraging four-letter words and one-finger waves. I guess I was parked more on the road than the shoulder. I recall crumpling over the center console to hit the hidden switch that activated the blue lights. The last thing I wanted was to get rear ended, or a uniformed cop rolling up to find me like that. It was humiliating.

I was so ashamed of the things I'd said in front of my brothers. My sweet son and his innocent mother deserved so much better than that. I wanted to be a good husband and dad, but no matter how I tried, I failed. It was like some dark force was controlling my thoughts.

I constantly tried to reassure myself that I wasn't going nuts, but there was no explanation for my excessive drinking, foul language, multiple anonymous sex partners, or the verbally abusive telephone conversations with my son's mom. I wasn't raised to be that way.

It had to have been job stress. After all, it was New Orleans in the nineties. It was possibly the most dangerous city in America at the time, and the most corrupt police department. The FBI had wiretapped the entire NOPD. I was carrying federal credentials in a city crawling with dirty local cops. My job was to bust drug organizations and avoid having my cover revealed by the dirty cops. Yeah, it had to be the stress of the job.

It wasn't.

Introduction

I'd labeled myself as broken and good for nothing but chasing down violent criminals like an animal. I knew it took one to catch one. In my heart, I was falling apart because I'd lost my marriage and family. In my head, I knew what I wanted to do, but ego and anger stopped me from doing it. But why?

I was guilty, dead, and buried in my sin, but I was too stubborn to stop and surrender to Christ. I was going to fix it all by moving on and making things better with my newest girlfriend. Well, as if you haven't already figured out how that went, I married again on the rebound. After one and a half months, we were done. After eighteen years of more child support, we were finally done.

That was over twenty years ago, and oh, how I'd love to tell you once the second divorce ended, I put my life back on the rails and sailed smooth into the golden years. But I'd be lying to you. While my professional career skyrocketed like a stellar LinkedIn profile, my personal life remained mired in rejection, abandonment, addiction, and consistently crappy choices.

The kicker about sin is while we can be restored if we repent and ask forgiveness, there are still consequences. Some consequences take the form of alimony, child support, or a rental home while joint property is liquidated. Others attack our ego—public exposure, humiliation, loss of respect and career. Still others have a more serious and permanent effect such as addictions, disease, and death.

My troubles didn't start with my first marriage. They began as a kid. I grew up Godless, in the shadow of a dominant, detached father. His physical intimidation and control through silence left me without ever having heard a kind word, seeing an interest in my life, or speaking the words, "I love you."

Family dysfunction screws up a lot of us, and the messed-up part is that we go years without a clue that how we were raised wasn't the way things were supposed to be. All we know is what we know. But that doesn't make it right. It just makes us hurt. To this day there is nothing I could've done to prevent or change

Introduction

history. But I did have the opportunity to define my response in the present. I decided to heal, and then God led me to share so you can heal too.

In case you were wondering about that day in New Orleans on the shoulder of the road, no I didn't die (obviously). Instead, I placed myself into a coffin called guilt, held a funeral called pain, and buried myself in a grave called shame. It wasn't until God's mercy and grace raised me up, brushed me off, and gave me the key to freedom from my past that I was able to live again.

I have that key, and I want to give it to you.
Scott

1

FINDING FREEDOM

So if the Son sets you free, you will be free indeed.
John 8:36

* * *

It's still clear as a bell. I was so excited and nervous as I filled out the application for a local sheriff's office in the late 1980s. Oddly enough, there were no check boxes asking if I wanted to be a good cop or bad cop. Not even multiple-choice questions about suicide, divorce, alcoholism, domestic violence, drug abuse, committing petty theft, or major corruption.

There were no requirements that I be or become socially cynical, emotionally detached, or personally uncaring. I wasn't even asked to write a paragraph about becoming disenfranchised with the ideals of public service or joining other officers in a cultural divide against the people we swore to protect and serve.

So how and why do so many idealistic first responders become entrenched in a cycle of personal destruction while trying to do a job that helps protect others from the things often caused by the very pain we harbor inside?

Most officers are too busy hopping from one radio call to the next to stop and ask why. Why is the socialization process for first responders so mystical, so secretive, and so misunderstood, as to unravel past personal pains buried deep inside for years?

I've got your six—I want to help you understand that what you're experiencing didn't start the day you swore the oath. It also didn't begin with the last tragedy you witnessed. Past personal pain is a path often traced back to your childhood and family relations. It's not unusual for us to never understand or become aware of what harm was done because it was the life we knew. *All you know, is what you know.* Right?

I served almost twenty-six years in law enforcement before retiring as a chief of police. In those years, I was assigned to federal and state multi-jurisdictional task forces alongside officers and military personnel. Throughout sixteen years in SWAT special operations, I've trained, worked, and agonized with firefighters, hazmat techs, and EMTs.

My career has shown me that no matter the uniform patch, we all serve the same flag while suffering the same pain. Personal hurt is a badge of honor among the fraternity. It's expected. But this white albatross isn't honorable, nor is it necessary. It's become the cultural norm because we know no other way out except for addiction or suicide. Not even retirement spares us from the hurt.

Like most of you, I wear more scars on the inside than on the outside. I've been there, and through all of those years, I'd come to accept my exit strategy. I called it, "In Case Of," and it was the Colt Python .357 revolver I kept in the nightstand by my bed. It never saw the inside of my duty holster because it was there to serve only one purpose. It wasn't until I was freed from the bondage of my past that I finally unloaded it. It was no longer an option.

During those years, every wound threatened to destroy me, damage my reputation, and drain my life of joy that God created me to know. It took years before I learned that my life of constant misery was a result of my past pain, and that I could be freed from it.

I was so desperate to find out why I lived the way I did, that I devoted years of my life researching and writing my doctoral dissertation on cop culture. I thought I'd found the key to my freedom once my work was published. I declared my acting out was a by-product of the first responder lifestyle. A noble cost we paid to serve the public who so desperately needs our rescue.

What truth I came to know, was that I was looking at the wrong book. Sure, my work was successful in documenting police organizational culture and the effects of becoming blue, but I was missing the target. I was missing the real truth that God was the answer. His book held every key I sought for breaking free from my life of past personal pain.

I want to hand you the key to your freedom.

Our fraternity speaks a different language. Even our spouses don't understand the hushed conversations and innuendoes, but the message remains the same. If you are married, engaged, or teetering on the abyss of divorce, please share this with your loved one. Believe it or not, they suffer just as you do, and sometimes possibly worse. You get to handle the situation. They can only stay home and worry about what it is you're handling. And not handling.

Trust me, there is a better way, and I'm so thankful you've joined me for this journey. If you have been, or are still, trapped in the bondage of pain and shame, this is where we work together to gain permanent freedom.

For decades, I struggled with the effects of past pain. I knew nothing about the reality that pain carried forward, or that it would continue to create problems in my life. I mistakenly figured what was in the past was in the past. If problems lingered, then it was my fault for not getting over it, or even worse, being soft.

. . .

Although in my head I wanted to change, I didn't have the tools to make it happen. I knew I was hurting, and eventually began to accept the fact that I must be broken and of no value.

Like you, I'm a rational person skilled in the art of managing crisis situations and fixing other people's problems. Yet I couldn't understand why I acted out and made such poor personal choices. It's like trying to untangle headphone cords. The more you pull and struggle, the more tangled they become. Mine were in a knot, and I'm guessing yours are too.

My work was pristine. I'd labor over the content of an inner-office email until the tone and tenor were just right. Yet my personal life was chaos. Twice divorced, strained relationships with my kids, more child support than I could afford, and constantly running from one barroom brawl and relationship to another.

I wanted to change, but I honestly thought I was losing my mind because no matter how hard I tried to "be good," I'd do the opposite. Damaged goods was what I called myself for decades. I didn't deserve happiness, was what I thought. I had allowed my past to define my present, and the curse of pain to steal the joy of freedom.

When we talk about pain, we first think of physical pain from injury or accident. Because of our alpha attitudes toward fixing society's problems, we don't invest much time worrying about that pain or the recovery. How many of us returned to duty or the office mere days after serious injury? It's like our healing center. We don't focus on the emotional angle of hurting. How could we; we're first-responding heroes after all!

That was my stubborn mindset for years but thank God for the revelation that my unresolved pain was devastating and held a lasting effect on my life. Even more thanks to God for showing me the path to freedom from the stranglehold of what living a life of hurt and hate had caused.

. . .

Broken and Blue

I was blessed by His mercy and want to share God's word and my journey toward liberation from what had devastated so much of me for so many years. Sure, I know it's not alpha to open up about being weak or confess areas of pain and guilty darkness. I played that game of suck it up, and what I discovered was:

1. Being tough and being healthy are two very different things.
2. Suffering in silence holds no honor.
3. The co-workers' opinions you care so much about today, mean zilch unless they care about your well-being.
4. You are commissioned by God to heal from the pain of your past.
5. You are no good to anyone else until you're good to yourself.

Here's to you finding freedom from your past.

Call To Action

1. Write out what you think is meant by past personal pain.
2. Write out a list of what past pains still hurt you.
3. Write out a list of anyone who has caused you to hurt in your past.
4. Write out a detailed example of how a past pain still causes struggle today.

2

DEFINING PERSONAL PAIN

Now the Lord is the Spirit, and where the Spirit of the Lord is, there is freedom.
2 Corinthians 3:17

* * *

Identifying past pain for first responders is usually a tough job. It's like that itch you just can't seem to scratch or the word on the tip of your tongue. It's there and has an effect on you, but it's nothing you can touch, taste, or tangibly describe. Whatever it is, it's just there.

Too often it gets mixed in with trauma from the job. We fail to understand the distinction between what's currently causing stress and the deep-rooted pain of PTSD that resurfaces with each horrific call for service at work.

For the few who see the difference between work stress and past pain, the extent of how each affects you may not be so evident. Despite the variations of our personal experiences with past pain, we have a horrible habit of not addressing it.

Before we begin to dig down to discover the source of our own hurt, I'm going to do you a huge favor by telling you about a lie that almost all of us have been fed. It's also something we've clung to it as if it's the gospel truth. You ready?

Time does NOT heal all wounds.

There, I said it. While it may not have instantly changed your life, it is an important block on which we'll build this challenge for gaining freedom. Why is it so important? Because it's what we as a first responder culture have accepted, and there's an unrealistic expectation for time to actually heal all wounds. Thankfully, today more agencies are accepting of post-traumatic incident debriefings. They help us process what our minds and emotions are trained to suppress. But like dirt under the rug, the junk doesn't go away with time.

I spent decades wondering what was wrong with me. I beat myself up because I thought it was weak to suffer with guilt over people I'd hurt and failures like divorces and broken relationships with my sons. I lugged around shame for feeling sadness, hurt, and anger about growing up in a dysfunctional, Godless home without love or kindness.

Later in life, the stripes of a childhood spent in the turmoil of emotional rejection and abuse prevented me from sharing normal relationships with others. It all fell apart when I couldn't show affection to my wife. Labeling yourself as broken can sometimes become a self-fulfilling prophecy.

I say junk because that's what it is today. It's just junk that I had no control over back then, and it has no value in my life now. It's junk, and like any pile of trash, if it isn't properly disposed of it'll rot until the stench becomes unbearable.

Heroes, we're not going to wait on time to heal anything any more than we're going to stand by during an active shooter or burning building. This is where we do what we do best—we take action and work hard to gain our own healing through the restorative power and grace of Jesus Christ.

So what is past pain, and how exactly are we going to work toward being freed from it? That's a great start and defining what it is will be your personal journey. Getting and staying away from it is where we work like shift partners to get there.

Sources and causes for our past pain may result from cases of neglect, abuse, abandonment, parents' divorce, our own divorce, broken relationships, traumatic loss or death, being bullied, school issues, self-esteem, puberty, sexual identity, gender confusion, serious illness or disease, or any of the many things that get under our skin and clamp down until we feel as though we've lost control.

It's important that if you haven't already identified what it is that haunts you, to really begin praying over this. Ask God to reveal to you what it is in your spirit that you need to be freed from. These bonds that tether us to past events and people are called soul ties. You have the supernatural authority to cut those ties.

While soul ties can be positive bonds to old friends and family (*1 Samuel 18:1*), they are also spiritual attachments to events, actions, images, or anything that has trapped you in that moment in time that just won't allow you to be free to move forward with your life. Sort of like the weekend shift!

Some first responders visualize these spiritual ties as strands, like spider webs stretching from that moment in the past to where they are today. When I began to understand the concept of soul ties, I immediately saw my past pain connected to my spirit by giant suspension bridge cables.

It might sound funny if this is your first exposure to the reality of soul ties, but once you begin to pray over them, you will start to "see" yourself still supernaturally connected to your past. Like I said, mine were so powerfully destructive over the course of my life that they were like thick, impenetrable cables. But, as I prayed God's authority over them, they were sliced like a hot KA-BAR through butter.

Too often, we also just blow it off. Most of us don't like going to a doctor when we're sick or hurt because we figure it'll go away, or we can deal with it. Past personal pain is the same way. Can you live with guilt and shame? Sure, you can. Until you can't.

Outside of suicide, which is our final, most desperate effort to stop the hurting, we turn to medicating the negative effects. Consider your own methods of dealing with harmful issues. While not everything we do is as destructive as suicide, the effort is often driven by a need to ease the injury.

I'll give you an example of someone you know. Me.

I grew up in a home dominated by a very intimidating father. He never said he loved me, or liked me, or for that matter never said anything nice at all. I grew up telling myself that he was just the strong, silent type of father who showed his love instead of expressing it. The truth was, outside of food, shelter, and rides to ball practice, there was no showing of affection.

I didn't realize how his rejection had affected my entire life until the obsessions of overcompensating, sexual addiction, and consistent bouts with sadness, depression, and desperation almost kept me down on the canvas.

What did I do? I toiled my entire life looking for that acceptance. We all have an innate desire to be accepted, affirmed, and loved. I don't care how tough you are, we were all created by God with the need for relationships. I grew up without a model for a healthy one, so I stumbled from one bad relationship to the next for decades.

The pain I carried dominated my life and the decisions I made without even understanding what was going on. While I fixated on every aspect of building a successful public persona in my profession, I'd abandoned all hope for peace in my personal life. Living a double-minded existence like James 1:8 mentions isn't what we were designed to do.

. . .

The point is, we can muddle through life without ever scratching that itch, or we can rid ourselves of it, and move forward with living the blessed life that God created for us.

Call To Action

1. Write out in detail everything that you are aware of that has caused you past pain.
2. Write out a pledge to cut yourself free from the tethers of past pain and forgive those who have hurt you.

3

AVOIDING PAST PAIN

"I have the right to do anything," you say—but not everything is beneficial. "I have the right to do anything"—but I will not be mastered by anything.
1 Corinthians 6:12

During my career, I commanded a large, nationally accredited investigations bureau at a Louisiana sheriff's office. One case in particular required all of the resources of my division. Detectives, juvenile investigators, narcotics agents, and SWAT were all rallied together to solve this case. Although we knew without a doubt the person was guilty of heinous sex crimes against children, we never made an arrest.

Why?

Because none of his victims would testify against him.

We'd painstakingly researched numerous civil lawsuit settlements that named the minor-aged boys he molested. Of course, money settlements were what stopped the boys' parents from filing criminal charges a decade earlier. But there was no statute of limitations and we now had victims to back up what was being reported.

We were determined to make criminal cases against this serial sexual offender. By now, all of the male victims had grown to be men. When approached, they shut us down cold. Men would rather suffer in silence than face the potential of pain, shame, or humiliation in confronting past injuries head on.

I grieve for those victims. Although in their shame, they remained silent, their lives were lived in public turmoil. Addictions, divorce, and arrests were just some of the consequences of hiding what was done to them as children. I never judged them, and today I understand even more about why they locked down their past.

While not all past pain is caused by sexual abuse, the point is, we're first responders who clean out other people's dirty laundry, so we don't dare air out our own. In a culture where we've accepted the mantle of society's moral entrepreneurs, the risk of exposure to even our most trusted friend or a professional counselor is not worth the chance of losing face in the macho department.

Let's take a look at some of the deeper reasons we avoid exposing our pain to a healing light. Of course, our culture encourages first responders to endure as much pain as humanly possible without showing it. To do so is to show weakness and to be much less of a hero. Because society is expected to celebrate bravery and selfless service, showing cracks in that armor is akin to failure.

Like I said, that is the culture within which we live. It's not right, but it is what we've allowed it to be. So why would we rather crash and burn than heal? To start, first responders are fixers and doers. We hammer way too many nails and drive far too many miles in the wrong direction just to avoid asking for directions. It's the way we were genetically inclined.

Before we begin to blame God for creating us this way, the reality of being a fixer and a doer is not a bad thing. It's actually how and why we've survived in the toughest professions on earth. Unfortunately, like too much of a good thing, we allowed risk-taking to become defined primarily by our ability to fix it, do it, and endure it. We find nobility in helping others without first helping ourselves.

We are also driven by ego, and that is a major factor in our avoidance of help. The right ego is important to the alpha hero. An attack on our ego by showing a need for help is interpreted as a diminished ability. Humility is on very limited display when ego is running the show.

In the years that I suffered most, there were people who cared about my well-being. They recognized that I needed help. But, in the public position I held, and by operating within an occupational culture of cops, seeking help meant a threat to my esteem, status, and definitely my pride.

I defiantly chose to suck it up and reinforce the façade that shielded my weaknesses. While avoiding it allowed me to navigate a career, suffering came to a head where I knew an implosion was imminent. I was taking greater risks for much less return, and the deeper I fell into despair, the more desperate I became for anything to numb my pain. When or how the implosion would occur, I didn't know, but it was coming.

Because of my childhood, I struggled with deep-seated rejection. I needed to feel wanted, and good enough to be accepted. Possibly even be loved. Yeah, I know. We're all so tough, but the truth is, we all have a desire to be loved. That desire for love was originally aimed at God to fulfill, but over the generations we've assumed it was a need we could fill on our own. We were wrong.

After my second divorce, I remained single about twenty years. Those marriages failed because of my struggles with past pain from an unhealthy family foundation while growing up. So in my desperation for acceptance, I dated a lot of women. Well, to be honest, it wasn't as much about dating as it was about physical sex.

Sex numbed the darkness for about as long as it took to complete the act. Then, I'd lie there next to a disconnected partner feeling worse about myself than I did after the last sexual encounter. The problem was, the lower I felt, the more I needed the temporary fix. It wasn't the cure, but it was better than the revolver waiting in my nightstand.

Operating in a secret environment while serving in a public position was just a matter of time until the two worlds collided. Although I justified my actions as being single, and doing what single guys did, I knew inside it was much more problematic than that. I was hurting, and sex was the medication I used to mask the pain. I needed healing, not placating.

Many people don't understand the mentality of "all or nothing." As first responders, we seek ways of not hating or blaming ourselves so much, so we must go for it all in everything we do. There's no happy medium. If/when a situation ends in a mess, then there's no consideration for retooling for repair and recovery. It becomes an issue of nothing.

The problem occurs when the contrived image of control implodes—emotionally wounded first responders aren't hesitant to commit suicide. It's rationalized as better to fall on the sword than being publicly exposed as having had a personal problem we couldn't fix ourselves.

Terminating life over living with a lost reputation shares an odd equality among first responders. We often rationalize suicide as not only ending the pain, problems, and public exposure, but that our broken lives weren't worth the effort of collecting the pieces to repair.

Attempted suicide among first responders is ten times that of the general population according to a report of the *Journal of Emergency Medical Services*. Despite the need, the number of available resources reflect that the fraternity's agencies have a lack of understanding or willingness to help. For example, only 3 to 5% of America's 18,000 law enforcement agencies have suicide prevention training programs.

The air of dominance becomes a major factor in why first responders refuse to seek help. There's the misconception we were placed on this earth to dominate it with an aggressive, conquering iron fist. Genesis 1:26 describes God's authorization to have dominion over all things on earth. It was reaffirmed through Noah as well, but there is no commissioning to lord over it all. We are called to care for, nurture, and multiply. That command to care for also applies to caring for ourselves.

Our stubborn, self-reliant, nose-to-the-grindstone characteristics of alpha heroes can create challenges for us. When not taken to extremes or balanced with self-care, awareness, and compassion, our alpha characteristics can be good qualities to get us through when times get tough. But, the flip side, it also stops us from asking for what we need most—help.

Some other factors that stop us from healing are discussed below. No one wants to admit to being a victim. Victimhood implies someone overcame us, and we were incapable of defending ourselves or others. We see the role of needing protection as that of civilians.

If we've been victimized, then it shows we weren't strong enough, smart enough, or good enough to fight off an attack from a more dominant force. That failure is best hidden in our wounded spirit where the consequences continue to torment us long after the threat of being the victim has passed.

Failure is not an option for most first responders. After all, who wants to fail? We place value in our ability to succeed regardless of whom it affects or how we define success. I still recall the television character of Al Bundy. I bet you could tell me how many touchdowns he scored in one football game. Poor guy's greatest achievement occurred one Friday night decades ago, but that was and remained his definition of success. But he was a fictional character. Sure, so how many of us feel who we are right now was defined by what we did back then? Not so fictional now, is it?

Are we stuck in the past because the future only threatens us with the pain that occurred back then? Are we living our lives below the radar because we know how fragile we actually are without getting help? Are we so afraid of being seen as a failure that we've chosen to live a lie? Failure is not getting knocked down. It's refusing to get back up. We teach it in the academies, so why don't we believe it applies to every aspect of our lives?

As I wrap up this section about why first responders refuse to deal with the pain from our past, I want to circle back to the beginning story of the criminal investigation of the serial child molester.

Not all past pains stem from sexual sin, but many do. Whether it's molestation, abuse, rape, pornography, early exposure or experimentation, or a general confusion created by an absence of adult guidance, many first responders experience problems based on these and other issues related to sex.

One of the final factors that stop us from seeking help with our pain is being seen as less than sexually capable or homosexual. The many victims we'd interviewed during that criminal case were heterosexual and some are now married. They had no intention of opening a can of worms that included an illegal, same-sex encounter.

Understand that your maturity and mentality level at that age does not define who you are today. Whether it was forced upon you, or you were youthfully curious in your experimentation, the young you does not define the current you. Is there forgiveness and forgiving required for moving forward? There usually is, and if so, you must pursue that. But it's critical to remember you are not condemned to live a secret life of pain, shame and guilt.

In 2 Corinthians 5:17, God assures us that we are new creations in Christ, and that the old man falls away. Brothers and sisters, there is no need to continue living with darkness hidden in your life. It will take the light of Jesus Christ to begin the healing and restoration of your joy.

Call To Action

1. Write out whether or not you are open to receiving help in healing from past pain. If not, write as if explaining to your most loved ones why you refuse help to heal.
2. Write out what you would want help in healing to look like.
3. Write out how your life would look if you were living without the things that haunt you.

4
MANAGING PERSONAL PAIN

You, my brothers and sisters, were called to be free. But do not use your freedom to indulge the flesh; rather, serve one another humbly in love. [14] For the entire law is fulfilled in keeping this one command: "Love your neighbor as yourself."
Galatians 5:13-14

* * *

What's really eating away at you? Are regrets consuming your thoughts, so much so that you're forced to constantly shut them down? Can you sit in silence without a mental movie flooding your brain and demanding that you fill the quiet space where unhealthy thoughts roam free?

Does the last duty shift ricochet in your thoughts, or is it the faces of those you simply cannot help? How about this: does the last argument or rejection by a supervisor continue to play out in mental scenarios until it becomes twisted into a fantasy of revenge?

. . .

You're not alone. The pain we carry from our past is tucked away and always available to muck up our lives or turn gold star moments into brown star regrets. We allow pain, shame, and regret to overwhelm us with stress over how to cope with it. Unfortunately, the coping solves nothing. Healing does.

Have you developed your own secret way of helping to ease that hurt? Does your way involve something that if exposed, would embarrass you, ruin your reputation, or cost you a career? If so, then you are not working toward healing, you are enabling the hurt.

Concealing our weakness and our unhealthy ways of dealing with it is a common practice for first responders. We avoid dealing with all types of pain, from physical ailments to emotional trauma. Is it good for us? Not always. But it's what we do. Our natural inclination that "I can handle it" squeezes out God's supernatural ability. By avoiding God, and not trusting Him to provide for restoration, we multiply the problems as we head out and away from His will.

Why do we avoid God? Because the devil whispers in our ear that we're not worthy, and we can't trust God because all He wants to do is convict and punish us. If you haven't figured this out yet, the devil is the father of lies (John 8:44) and binding you to your past pain is his gain.

I will assure you that there is no other way to be freed from the pain of your past than through Jesus Christ, the great healer and physician. I was there. I know full well what you're going through. Remember, I was the one that kept "In Case Of" next to the bed for twenty years.

I wish so bad that there was a cool movie production to show you the hell I went through before I found healing. No matter how I describe it, there just aren't words to tell you how much dragging myself through each day really sucked. Knowing I was better than the decisions I made, but still making stupid choices before it was all said and done.

. . .

First responders are trapped with a double whammy. Traditional consequences usually fail to "scare" or deter us from behaving bad, and because we operate within a "golden halo" we worry less about the potential for getting caught. We always naturally assume someone will have our back before it gets too bad. And honestly, the only real consequence we worry about is losing our precious job.

Because we work within the system, there's also that buzz of gaming the system. Weighing risk versus reward before taking action allows us to consider the worst-case scenario through our handy, carnal risk assessment matrixes. Along with kicking the can down the road, we like to think we're getting away with not asking for help. God gives us biblical examples and consequences of how avoiding Him only drags out the injury. There are three primary ways we try to manage pain on our own.

David

King David was exalted as a great and mighty ruler. God Himself chose David to be king over Israel because of what He saw on the inside (1 Samuel 16:7). Although David was anointed by God, he didn't come to the throne without serious personal baggage. David is a lot like us in carrying personal pain from our past.

David did as good of a job as he could with avoiding what troubled him, but like us, it eventually became too much to bear and soon cost him dearly. The example of David is used because he engaged in one of the most common types of methods for dealing with past pain. Instead of addressing what issues in his past caused him so much hurt, David began to medicate his pain.

There are many ways to ease our pain. Some of us use alcohol, drugs, sex, exercise, work, or any of many addictions to compensate for the hurt we feel from an emptiness caused by an unresolved pain.

Because David preferred to seek a temporary fix instead of a permanent solution, he used what we refer to as **medication** in unsuccessfully dealing with pain. David's medication of choice was the flesh. His sexual addiction caused problems for everyone associated with him. David's family suffered greatly because of his sexual sin, and a generational curse was cast upon his children.

David's pain was rooted in the rejection by his father, Jesse. He wasn't considered worthy of meeting the prophet Samuel who was sent by God to anoint a ruler. Yet, there in that rejected, messed-up boy, Israel had a king. David's rejection by his father stung and stuck. Have you been hurt by a parent, and never forgiven them? This injury doesn't heal in time.

I'll share that as a kid way back in the seventies, I'd gotten a red warm-up suit with white stripes. It looked just like the one worn by my hero, Steve Austin, The Six Million Dollar Man (not the wrestler). I wore it everywhere.

One day my dad called out to me, but I was mixing it up with the neighborhood kids and didn't hear him. Then his words became very clear: "Hey, idiot in that red suit, I'm talking to you." I was about ten years old. I stuffed that tracksuit in the trash, and forty years later, those words still hurt.

Solomon

The son of David, Solomon was by far the wealthiest and most wise human ever to grace the earth. Despite being born out of the scandal between his father, David, and the sexual affair he had with a married woman, Bathsheba, Solomon was loved by God and blessed tremendously.

The generational curse David incurred upon his family because of his failure to address past pain caused personal suffering for his son also. Solomon's wounds, as a result of family sin and the shame caused by the sexual affair of his father and mother, drove him to compensate in a very different way than David's medication.

. . .

Motivation and achievements were Solomon's failed attempt to soothe his pain. The more he accumulated the less he felt deserving. In Ecclesiastes 2 he shares the futility of trying to outwork his hurt. Take the time to read all of Chapter 2:1-24.

This is so personal to me, as I suspect it is to many of you. One of my first partners on the job was a good guy. We'll call him Jim. But to be honest, he could be a bit overbearing. As a rookie deputy, I struggled to purchase my duty weapon and all of the tools of the trade as I'm sure we all did. But this guy had the best, most current and outrageously expensive gear imaginable. As a matter of fact, he owned two and three of everything.

Was he wealthy? No, he was probably worse off than me, but he needed to feel like the word he used to describe his latest weapon, motorcycle, or girlfriend: "Elite."

He conquered everything he touched, except the ability to humble himself to God's will for healing from his past. Just below the tanned surface of rippling muscles were the tatters of a severely wounded soul. He'd been the victim of sexual abuse as a child, and his broken spirit drove him to over-portray manliness.

Along the way, he also suffered from divorce, bankruptcy, fathering a child in the course of an affair, and was eventually squeezed out of law enforcement. Still, he chose to rely on himself for getting out of a jam. Avoiding true healing and spiritual freedom through God's grace and mercy dooms us to an unending effort of emptiness and unsatisfactory results.

Our spirit requires peace, not prizes.

Absalom

There is a third unhealthy way of dealing with our hurt. Absalom was David's son and Solomon's half brother. His pain, like many with a dominant parent, began at home. Absalom also suffered from intense guilt over doing nothing to defend his sister from a sexual attack by another half brother.

How often do we find ourselves in a situation we know is wrong, yet we sit by as injustice unfolds? Acts of abuse or unfair treatments occur among families and friends. Being a victim or witness causes pain that if not resolved will continue to fester. This is especially true for acts of policy and legal violations we witness on duty yet feel powerless to report it.

Meditation stewed in Absalom's spirit as hatred intensified. For two years he avoided confronting his feelings and the offender before it erupted, and he killed his half brother.

Absalom's deep-seated pain directed against his father, King David, also caused him to try overthrowing his reign. Absalom's desire to destroy his father led to his own death. Attacks against others is what defines Absalom. Are you feeling the rage of regret and wrongdoings roil beneath the surface while you look for an outlet to unleash your fury upon?

Which One Are You?

Do you booze it until you lose it, yet it's worse than it began? Please understand that the substances used to fight addiction are not the problem. The problem is you're using addictive substances to avoid healing from your pain.

Brothers and sisters, drinking, screwing around, and fighting will not heal your hurt. Don't listen to the devil. God's not waiting to smack you like a carnival game of whack-a-mole. You are good and you are worthy to be loved. God wants to heal you because He loves you.

Allow yourself to heal. It's better than the hurt.

God placed a message on my heart a few years ago that remains with me today. "Avoiding is not winning." I love that old saying, "You can run from the police, but you'll just go to jail tired." You know there's a problem. Otherwise you wouldn't be reading this book. It's time to stop avoiding healing and get serious about the long-term solution. Whether it requires confessing a wrong to a friend, spouse, co-worker, or forgiving yourself for messing up once again, don't put off gaining the freedom from your past that you deserve.

Call To Action

1. Write out which of the three examples are you most like (Medication, Motivation, or Meditation).
2. Write out ways you've developed to ease or cope with your past pain.
3. Write out the personal, professional, and social consequences if someone exposed your coping mechanisms.

5

OUR PAST REMINDS US, NOT DEFINES US

But Scripture has locked up everything under the control of sin, so that what was promised, being given through faith in Jesus Christ, might be given to those who believe.
Galatians 3:22

* * *

I don't think there's any disagreement about whether our earlier life plays a role in influencing who we are today. Not only do genetics through DNA influence us on an individual level, but society, culture, and experiences play important roles in shaping who we are.

We're out of luck changing our DNA, but we have God's full authority to become redefined in His light through Jesus Christ. Now, with that encouraging piece of information, let's look at what and why we might want to make changes to who we are, and how we came to be that way.

Going back to our earliest days of childhood, bad experiences usually have a profound effect on how we behave as an adult.

Dysfunctional family dynamics are the most common cause of persistent adult pain. Unhappiness or trauma during a child's most formative years has the potential for causing tremendous scarring as they become an adult.

Maybe it was an alcoholic parent, or a family member who subjected others to physical, mental, or sexual abuse. Parents suffering with depression leave impressions of abandonment on their kids, although they may be physically in the same home. I'd be willing to bet that most of us had at least one dominant parent in the house.

Past pain can and often does push beyond emotional barriers until it affects you physically, psychologically, and spiritually. This surrounding of turmoil also creates an unhealthy environment for those related or associated with you.

Unrecognized past personal pain may evolve into chronic mental disorders such as states of depression, anxiety, and PTSD (post-traumatic stress disorder). Living in a state of chaos, whether real or perceived, places the brain in a red zone of self-defense. Do you feel like no one likes or respects you? How about the feelings that your job is in jeopardy or that someone is trying to take your position away from you?

I'm not talking about wearing a tinfoil hat while taping newspapers over your windows, but I am talking about the effects of darkness in your life. Without realizing it, you may be placing your job, your marriage, or your family at risk. If your pain is driving you to drinking, drug use, porn consumption, or any number of reactions beyond what is healthy, then you might just have someone after you and your job.

The reality is that while you are oppressed beneath the pressure of darkness in your spirit, your instincts can become dulled by the persistent internal agony. Your brain will also rewire as a result of the constant state of discomfort. Through the process of neuroplasticity, the brain protects and prepares itself based on past and current data.

Once you are aware that there is an issue, although you may not know what it is or where it began, you can be sure that your body has already begun the transformative process of self-preservation. This is why it's so important at this point where you've made a commitment to heal, that you follow through on that effort. If you saw a wanted felon, and gave chase, you wouldn't stop for no reason, would you?

There are an unlimited number of scenarios with the potential for causing harm to you as a child. There are also varying degrees of severity for how any one or a combination of factors influence who you become as an adult. The important thing to remember is that you are not to blame for what happened to you as a child, but you are responsible for how you choose to react to it as an adult.

We're here working together to understand why you continue to act out in a way that is harmful for you and possibly embarrassing as well. The majority of time, your irregular behavior, thoughts, and emotions can be traced back to trauma experienced in childhood. But let's also consider that pain experienced as an adult is just as influential as harm known as a child. After all, the jobs we do are unlike any other on the planet.

Sometimes the injuries are even more severe and impactful because we add the caveat of guilt for not knowing better as an adult or having been victimized by a trusted person. There is the added shame of being duped or hurt by another peer seen as your equal. So, you see, no one is immune to being harmed, but we can improve our ability to be restored if we focus on the healing instead of hurting or revenge.

Let's consider someone whose spouse cheated on them, or maybe they just abandoned the family. The thoughtless acts of an unfaithful spouse leave deep scars. It may also cause you to no longer trust the opposite sex because you see them as cruel and untrustworthy. Many of us then decide to either avoid commitment or hurt them before they hurt us. Whether or not they ever intended to hurt us, that is.

While childhood harm causes fear and instability, adult damage attacks confidence and self-esteem. Compensation takes a form of behavior that becomes as self-destructive as the core offense. Can you think through the ways we compensate for the pain, and how that influences who you are and how you behave?

It's not uncommon for the child of an alcoholic to become an alcoholic, or the child of a wife beater to abuse his own spouse. How about those who were sexually abused, and grow up with intimacy issues, gender confusion, or struggles with homo- or bisexuality. These are real problems, but just like the victims of that monster child molester I investigated, everyone stays silent about the pain. It will not just go away.

Once you drop the guarded defense, and stop making excuses, you'll begin to identify particular behaviors that are traceable to a point in the past. Whether that point was decades or weeks ago, it doesn't matter. What does matter is that you have the God-given authority to change that behavior by working to heal what has hurt you.

I'll end this with something wonderful that happened through my own healing. My wife had grown weary of a habit I had, but that I never realized I was doing. Anytime she reached out to touch me, I would either block it (gently) with a PPCT self-defense type technique or quickly pull away. She took that as me rejecting her pursuit and affection.

Her love language is touch, and like many women, she needs non-sexual, intimate touching throughout the day to reinforce the feeling of security that ultimately leads to intimacy. Instead, I'd turned us into a set of sparring partners with the only touching being my horseplay, or during sex.

Once God revealed the core cause of my defensive behavior, I understood that I was overly protective of being touched because intimacy, gentleness, and loving attention was not shown to me as a child. I saw physical contact as a threat to harm, direct, or control. It forced my body into a state of constant tension and alarm.

Eventually, as God began healing me, I was able to let down my guard and allow my wife in. Emotional, physical, and spiritual abandonment is common. The conflict is made more confusing when the parent(s) are in the home, but still avoid the familial connection of love, security, and significance.

If you are continuing to struggle with abnormal behavior or acting out, but don't know why, this is the perfect time to set your God goggles to re-examine your life to see the truth from your past. God isn't going to judge you for it. He loves you, and He knows the pain you suffered.

Dig deep into who you were to find out who you are. Please remember that it doesn't have to remain who you continue to be. The apostle Paul made it a daily practice to forget those things that are behind (Philippians 3:12), so that he could reach forward to pursue the life God blessed him with.

It's time to move forward.

Call To Action

1. Write out in detail one painful memory from your childhood.
2. Write out in detail one painful event from adulthood.
3. Write out how each of these may continue to be present and influence your behavior.
4. Write out a statement of commitment that releases you from the events and frees you to heal from all remnants of them.

6

SPIRITUAL FREEDOM

It is for freedom that Christ has set us free. Stand firm, then, and do not let yourselves be burdened again by a yoke of slavery.
Galatians 5:1

* * *

Spiritual Freedom

There are many definitions and descriptions for helping us to explain spiritual freedom. In the context of freedom from your past personal pain, let's talk about what it looks like for us first responders.

Past pain is harbored in the darkness of our hearts. We may not even realize it's hidden there, but this is why we're working together to identify it, and root it out. Let's assume that you have either recognized you have an issue with baggage from your past that is interfering with your present, or you have that persistent bug in your ear that something's just not right in your life.

Either of these are safe assumptions because you've invested in this challenge and are committed to slicing through the chains holding you down. While you can enjoy an intimate relationship with God through the salvation of Jesus Christ, there is still work to be done on clearing out the dark chambers in your heart. This is where resistance, pride, and pain reside.

I used to think freedom came as a result of control. The idea of surrendering to become free made no sense at all. There was no way I was going to surrender. I'd existed for years in my own suffering, I had continued to resist pulling "In Case Of" out of the nightstand, and I'd continued to advance in my career and education. I was in control of my destiny, and personal suffering was a price I was willing to pay.

But I wasn't in control. My addictions were driving that train and it was a matter of time until I launched it off the tracks and into a pit of destruction. Accumulation was one of my addictions. Gaining status, degrees, promotions, and winning at all costs were just some of the ways I tried (and failed) to escape the darkness in my life. Even when I became chief of police, that wasn't enough. I began applying to police chief notices at bigger agencies to fill the void of feeling significant.

Sitting at home alone set my mind on fire. I hated being by myself because rejection was painted all over it. There was no peace in my life. What made it worse was that I had to, and I mean had to, fight to keep it together while in the public eye. Any sign of weakness or crack in the armor would've signaled my demise. In hindsight, my seeking help would've probably allowed many others to do the same. The only way to eliminate darkness is by exposing it to light. The light of Christ is the remedy for the dark pain that causes you to stumble, sin, and separate yourself from God's loving will. Many of us think our pain is too deep to heal, but if you believe in God, then you know there is nothing, and I mean absolutely nothing, He cannot do.

. . .

A few lessons I learned in the wilderness of being apart from God's will are:

1. We didn't create the original problem.
2. We aren't responsible for what was done to us back then, but we are responsible for how we respond to it now.
3. We are not defined nor condemned by our past.
4. God gives us the authority to free ourselves from past personal pain.
5. God grants us the grace and blessing to live a blessed life.

Once I found peace in these truths, I began to peer deep into my past with what I called God goggles. My mind, heart, and head were open to the reality of re-examining my past. Not only things done to me, but also things I'd done to others and myself. We gain a Christ-like understanding when we pray for spiritual freedom from the chains that trap us in sin.

You can know spiritual freedom from the negative effects of past personal pain. God didn't create you to live a life below the radar. He loves you and wants you to know Him on an intimate level so that you'll trust Him enough to pursue His will for your life. The absence of spiritual freedom is a condition where past problems with continuing shame, blame, and guilt prevent you from being comfortable in God's presence.

Being free also means you are confident to openly live for God and exist in a state of transparency, trust, and accountability. This isn't to say that your business becomes everyone else's business, but a forgiving nature that is also forgiven allows you to move freely without the fear of exposure. There is nothing like having the shackles of fear, pain, and the always-present potential for exposure fall from your spirit. I want you to know the same feelings of confidence and freedom that I have discovered though Christ.

Call To Action

1. Write out a prayer for healing from past pain.
2. Write out what issues still remain in the dark chambers of your heart.
3. Have you surrendered everything to Christ? If not, write out what you are trying to hide and why is it so important to you.

7

LEARNING TO FORGIVE

In Him and through faith in Him we may approach God with freedom and confidence.
   Ephesians 3:12

* * *

Over thirty years ago, I made a traffic stop like the many other traffic stops rookies make. Except I was on a particularly desolate bayou country road with only limited communications with dispatch. There was no such thing as a police portable radio.

Two men bailed out of the car they were in, and the minor traffic violation escalated quickly. I immediately found myself outnumbered, and without backup. As I finally regained my senses, I noticed a van suddenly stop along the highway directly across from my cruiser. The driver jumped out and began running through the dark yelling at me. I recognized him as someone I had crossed paths with before, and I felt the heat of hatred begin to pump through my veins.

. . .

I ordered him back into his vehicle. He ignored me.

I recall yelling as loud as I could, "Leave now."

He continued to yell and curse at me and said, "I'll show you about leaving."

He spun back toward his van and threw the driver's door open. I was so keyed in on his aggression that I forgot about the other two guys. I think they were as shocked about what was happening as I was.

The man shoved his hand beneath the driver's seat. My heart was ramming against the inside of my chest. I knew my concealed body armor had to rise and fall with it. I'd drawn my duty weapon earlier, and now lifted it until my focus was fixed on his torso. I quit giving verbal commands and zeroed in on the sight picture at the end of my barrel.

I lost sight of his hands as they dug beneath his driver's seat. I began to apply pressure to the 9mm's trigger.

I recall holding my breath and a dread of what was about to play out over a traffic stop with a warning. And to top it off, he had nothing to do with it. But I knew once I shot this guy that all hell was going to break loose. I wasn't even out of the academy six months, and here I was about to make a decision that would change so many lives.

I'd taken the slack out of the trigger. He spun facing me. My vision shifted to his right hand that was coming out from beneath his seat. He was clutching an object. Dread had fully engulfed me as I pressed the air out of my lungs. The inside pad of my right finger felt the pressure of the curved trigger as I eased back against it.

The man squared toward me. In the light from his van's interior, I saw an object in his hand. Except that it was a glimpse of light brown, or tan. It didn't look right. I hesitated.

It was a pair of house slippers. I almost killed this man over a pair of house slippers. It was more emotionally draining than any on-duty shooting incident or serious injury. I hated this man almost thirty years because of the grief he caused over the highway confrontation.

Fast forward to my first year as chief of police, and my assistant buzzed to give me a heads up about someone demanding to see me. It was the very same man, and my assistant knew his reputation as well. I allowed him in, but this wasn't going to be the same nervous rookie along a back bayou road. But, much to my surprise, the adrenaline, the fear, and the hate came back as if I was back on that traffic stop.

Much older and frailer, he angrily launched into our meeting. He was making false allegations against one of my officers. When he handed me the citation, it wasn't even my agency that gave him the ticket. I was ready to throw him out. I was the chief and I'd had enough. Yes, I was no longer that rookie.

He tried to get out of the leather executive chair but struggled. I watched him struggle, and the hatred that raged inside encouraged me to delight in his helplessness.

He stopped struggling and leaned back. His yellowish eyes watered.

"I'm afraid to die," he whispered in tears.

"What?" My voice had lowered to match his.

"You're a good man, Scottie. I'm sorry for everything."

I didn't know what to say. I was happy, embarrassed, ashamed, and proud at the same time.

"You're dying?"

"I don't want to. I'm scared."

Once the scales of unforgiveness fell from deep inside me, I saw him. I mean really saw him. He was frail as he tugged at an adult diaper that had curled over his slacks. He was dying, and here I was reveling over his inability to get out of a chair.

The Holy Spirit came over me and I sprung up from behind my desk.

"Let's pray," I said. "Let's pray, now."

. . .

I helped him out of the deep chair, and we clasped hands tighter than I thought his trembling body could muster. My face sunk into his shoulder as I held his body upright while we both began to weep. Neither of us focused on the cancer. It was the prayers of healing that ran so deep for so long.

I asked God to forgive me and bless my brother with peace. I was thankful God brought him into my office and back into my life. I was moved so sincerely in prayer as I felt the weight of hate, the chains of anger, and the bitterness of unforgiveness fall from my spirit.

This meeting wasn't about a traffic citation; it was God allowing two broken spirits an opportunity to forgive. It was also about the power of reconciliation even after three decades.

Weeks later I was asked to attend his funeral. His family shared that he told them of our prayers, and that he'd come to peace over his passing that day in my office. For years, I hated this man, but God showed me that He dearly loves those who we may hate. And most importantly, that I should not be in the business of hating His loved ones.

This was a tough one to share for several reasons, but oftentimes saying "I love you" requires putting egos aside: mine. Those three decades that followed that one event were based on an unforgiving spirit, and an opportunity for reconciliation. I'm not proud of it, but I shared this because I don't want you to continue suffering from unnecessary past pain.

In order to progress toward healing, it's crucial that we understand the value of forgiving. Many first responders, myself included, spent years failing to consider what true forgiveness meant. We saw forgiveness as weakness. We looked at a sin or harm committed against us and wondered how we could possibly let the violator off the hook for what they did to us. Usually, we toiled over plots to get even. Becoming preoccupied with those thoughts allows darkness to access our minds.

. . .

Forgiveness is not about agreeing with or approving of what the violator did to us. Forgiving others is about setting ourselves apart from the hurt. Forgiveness allows us to be free from, not only the person who caused the harm, but the acts that injured us.

We witness so much evil in our jobs that it's easy to carry anger or hatred for those who hurt or kill others. Forgiveness isn't a commodity first responders naturally want to share with offenders. The posture of unforgiveness and grudge-holding erupts far beyond our tour of duty. It invades our personal relationships and causes stress for everyone involved.

It's easy to continue harboring hard feelings against someone who hurt us, but that anger is like poison we ingest while trying to hurt someone else. God is very clear about His demand that we forgive others. He carries it a step further, and declares that if we fail to forgive others, He will not forgive us (Mathew 6:14-15). Talk about motivation to come into a position of humble surrender! No grudge I held was ever worth so much as to separate myself from God.

So, what's this business about forgiving? It took me years of harboring grudges, hard feelings, and hatred toward others before I came to understand the blessing of forgiveness. Like many others, I might've said "I forgive you," to someone just to get them out of my face, but that was just paying lip service to move them along.

The truth of forgiving is that it's not for pacifying others. It is about our obedience to God's desire to live Christ-like. It's also about mirroring God's response to sin by forgiving us, so that we may separate the interference that unconfessed sin creates.

A guy I mentored, whom we'll call Chuck, was a police officer who also worked extra hours with a local ambulance service. He was embroiled in a longstanding feud with his siblings. As their mother drew closer to death, the fighting between brothers and sisters grew more intense, and the potential for physical harm escalated. As so many families experience, once their mother passed, they all began to fight over items and money in her will. It got bad—really bad.

After two years, and no settlement, Chuck reached out to me for help. His health was diminishing, his marriage was falling apart, and his faith was tested beyond anything he'd known. He'd stopped pulling shifts as an EMT because he couldn't handle the fatigue of extra hours.

I saw it in his face. He had to forgive his siblings. His initial reaction was what you can imagine. "No way. Do you know what they did to me?"

Yes, I knew exactly what they did to him. They'd hurt and disrespected him. For a first responder, respect is our language. Most of us don't mind talking, discussing, or arguing, but once the other person becomes disrespectful, it's over. Chuck was over it, except he was still suffering from the fallout of unforgiveness.

He may not have been engaged in the arguments or relationships anymore, but he was still very much involved. He was tied to them through an unforgiving spirit. Instead of freedom, he was trapped by them, and he was also separated from God's will and blessings. He felt completely isolated.

Chuck needed to know the truth, and he needed to put it into action immediately. His life depended on it. I shared the biblical truths of forgiveness and God's command to mirror His and Jesus's forgiving nature. Chuck was so wounded that he actually said he could never, ever forgive his siblings. He said it would take a miracle. What it would take was faith.

I assured him God already knew his heart and He wanted to hear Chuck's voice. He didn't even have to tell his siblings in person that he forgave them, he just needed to speak the words. Chuck said he began the process of speaking forgiving prayers out loud. First, he began while he showered because he didn't even want his wife to hear him. Next, his words of forgiveness occupied his work commutes. He'd say his siblings' names and that he forgave them. But to be honest, he said he didn't believe it.

After about a week, Chuck said each time he'd say a sibling's name in prayer, his anger at the sound of their name became less. He began to feel compassion for each one, as God shared the realities of why they acted out the way they did. In that, he also saw reasons from his past where pain drove his behavior toward them.

Eventually, Chuck said God placed the grace of mercy and forgiveness for his siblings in his heart, and immediately, Chuck noticed the hatred he carried had disappeared. He didn't know when it left, but he knew his heart was free. Soon, he was able to pray blessings over each sibling.

Chuck was at a point of seamless submission to God's will, and then he had a decision to make. He'd experienced the transition through forgiving and blessing without ever having to speak with his offending siblings. Now, he began to consider the possibility of restoring a relationship with them. God allows us authority when we forgive. We're not trapped with the offender, nor are we forced to endure their actions and behavior.

We can fully forgive someone, yet still have the authority to never speak with them again. I use the term pruning. In life there are relationships that suck positive, life-giving energy away from us, and ruin the possibility of new, nurturing relationships. Pruning is sometimes necessary so we are surrounded by affirming friends and family. But whatever you choose, God allows us the decision through free will.

Although he fully forgave them, Chuck chose to end the relationships with his siblings because their lives were filled with chaos and unteachable spirits that threatened the peace in faith God granted him. Chuck said God removed the desire for those relationships, and though he prays each comes to know Christ, he understands that he's not the one to lead them to Him.

One final hurdle that Chuck crossed was wanting to know about the consequences for his siblings who stole his mother's money and possessions even before the estate was settled. I knew there was still a seed of anger over those offenses. I helped him to understand that it was not his duty to punish his siblings for their sins.

They sinned against God by violating His laws. We have no authority to police on behalf of God. According to Romans 12:19, He's fully capable of handling violators on His own. Matter of fact, I'd much prefer God handle it.

So how does this relate to first responders? We will not, and I repeat, we will not ever know freedom from our past until we forgive those who have sinned against us.

Forgiving is Freedom; Unforgiveness is Captivity.

Unforgiveness

Our discussions about forgiveness can sometimes get confusing and slide off the rails when first responders get hung up on "letting their offender off the hook." I feel like we've covered the realities of God's command to forgive, and that the process is about setting you free from your offenders, while allowing God to take His vengeance.

Now let's talk about unforgiveness. It's pretty simple. If you do not forgive others, God will not forgive you (Matthew 6:15). I've been known to be pretty hardheaded in my life, but even I understand that.

Because God commands us to forgive, the fact that we either can't or won't is a direct attack on God's word. In other words, not forgiving is a sin, and a sin you will not be forgiven for because you've refused or failed to forgive others. Once we place ourselves into an environment of separation from God, there are a ton of adverse effects just waiting to happen. There is no neutral ground here, you are either covered by God's grace or controlled by Satan's reign.

This isn't the time to go all sad sack and ask, "Why me?" The answer isn't that God punishes us; it's that we've intentionally removed ourselves from beneath His hedge of protection and opened ourselves to the results of sin.

The solution is so simple. Forgive others as God has told us to do. It's not just so we'll do as He says, but it's a lifesaving and changing experience that draws us closer to the true heart of God's loving compassion. It's also the only way to genuinely change our heart toward others.

There is a negative power found with unforgiveness, and it has the potential to destroy you. Just to show you how serious this business is: God forgives all sin except for one. Mark 3:28-29 tells us that blaspheming the Holy Spirit is the single unforgivable, eternal sin.

God's not playing around when it comes to never forgiving someone who blasphemes the Holy Spirit, and He's equally serious about not forgiving those who refuse to forgive others. Either way, the outcome of not being forgiven is the same. The difference is, you do have the grace of God's covering, but you chose not to accept His gift.

For the wages of sin is death; but the gift of God is eternal life through
Jesus Christ our Lord.
Romans 6:23

Another simple truth is that sin brings death. Not automatically a physical death, but a separation from God. And because we do have the blessing of free will, we also have the ability to accept His gift of eternal life as opposed to the alternative. Seems like it's time to start forgiving those who have sinned against us.

I'd like to share a key example of how unforgiveness negatively affects us. Matthew 18:21-35 shares the conversation between Jesus and Peter in which they discuss forgiveness and how often must someone be willing to forgive. When and if we do forgive someone, most of us have the one-and-done attitude. Jesus has a very different number in mind.

Jesus also backed up His command of forgiving someone not seven times, but seventy times seven times. Now, before we write down 490, let's look at the historical reality behind that number. The tradition was that if you forgave someone three times, you were a very good person. Peter's question to Jesus included the traditional three, and he doubled it for good measure and added one to be sure. Seven times forgiven would surely make one a saint, right?

Seemed like everyone was trying to trip up Jesus, even His closest friends. Sound familiar?

Jesus gives the number seventy times seven not as a hard target, but to show that we never stop forgiving. Forgiving is a never-ending practice of mercy and grace. Just as Christ died for our sins once, His blood covers our sins for eternity. We are to forgive in all occasions and without limit or conditions.

Why? Because unforgiveness causes us pain. It also prevents us from escaping our past that caused the pain. If you were abused by a parent or adult, your refusal to forgive them keeps you shackled to that person and the harmful action. So unforgiveness not only puts us out in the cold from God's presence, but while out there, we're still attached to what hurt us in the first place. Not surprisingly, it's God that we need to set us free, but because we've turned from Him, we don't have the gift of His freedom-giving power.

God sacrificed His only begotten Son so that our sins would be forgiven once and for eternity. The example of forgiving is the greatest love sacrifice ever, and something we could never repay God. Yet, when He asks us to forgive one another, we balk because we've been harmed, or our feelings got hurt.

Don't misunderstand the negative power of unforgiving. It does cause pain and can lead to physical illnesses and emotional misery. It's sort of a pain prison where the ones we refuse to forgive are our jailers. They tug the chain, and we feel the pain. We can cut that invisible cord right this second by forgiving them.

Remember the three keys to genuine forgiveness:

1. Repent – Unforgiveness is a sin, so before forgiving those who have sinned against you, make the time to repent for your own sin of unforgiving.

2. Release – We've talked about judgments against others, and their effect on our own lives. To genuinely forgive, we must break the curse and release the judgment against others.

3. Bless – God is very clear that it's a two-step process. Not only must we forgive those who have sinned against us, but we must bless them.

Call To Action

1. Write out why you either cannot, will not, or refuse to forgive others.
2. Write out the names of three people who you need to forgive.
3. Write out separately in detail what each person's offenses were.
4. Write out a prayer of forgiveness for each person

8

REMAINING SPIRITUALLY FREE

I will walk about in freedom, for I have sought out your precepts.
Psalm 119:45

* * *

I've reached points in my life where I would beat a fist against the air and proclaim, "No more." The day of my declarations, I'd muscle through whatever it was I was going to stop, start, or change in my life. I was strong and committed—no problem.

The next day was the problem. Without a plan, I was lost in what to do and what to avoid. My natural, carnal desires would resurface, and just like that, I was wondering what had happened to my plan. Instead of relying on a foundation laid by the blood of Christ, I wallowed back into the behavior I'd just committed to stop.

This recurring pattern caused so much suffering during my career. Behind the badge, I was Johnny on the spot public servant, but alone, in my head, those addictive behaviors would rage against the public façade. Physical sex was always my go-to drug. I didn't realize how being rejected as a child would launch me into a search for acceptance and make-believe love. But, without fail, I'd vow to stop getting involved with the sin of unmarried sexual affairs and "get my life straight." Then, without God, I'd be back in bed and hating myself.

The binge-purge cycle is the same for any substance or addiction. It's why working for spiritual freedom is important. Although it's like anything from dieting to saving money—without a plan, failure is almost certain. I want to talk about several tactical ideas for helping you stay on the path. Like late-night snacks and adding extra pounds, we can just as easily fall back into the pain pool that has plagued us for years.

Let's start with the continual act of surrender. Some first responders see it as a contradiction of terms when we discuss freedom and surrender. We don't see how there can be freedom when giving up is usually associated with captivity. But we're talking about the spiritual realm of freedom and surrender.

Surrender

Surrender is not a word we easily embrace. To most of us, it means defeat, failure, or one of many negative words that offend us. While putting up a valiant effort and resisting the enemy is encouraged, surrendering our lives to Jesus Christ is the victory.

The act of surrendering to God is an act of love and trust. Sacrificial love is the highest expression there is. God gave up His one and only beloved Son so that we may know everlasting life through salvation. We are asked to sacrifice our sinful, selfish desires to God so that He may guide us to a relationship with Him and others.

Why doesn't God just *make* us listen and obey Him, you might ask? That's a great question. God loves us so dearly that He gave us free will. This is what separates us from the animals.

Unfortunately, free will is also what's caused us all of our troubles, beginning with Adam and Eve.

Just to take a step back into history, consider the very first couple ever created. Adam and Eve had it made. They literally lived in paradise and hung out with God every day. Yet they were given the grace to make their own decisions. God asked them not to eat from the fruit of the tree of knowledge of good and evil, and warned that if they did, they would surely die.

That sounds pretty simple to me, but they had every right to make their own choices despite their close relationship with God the Father. Guess what? They took a chance, and it caused them and us an eternal separation from God. This is why Jesus came to us as the final atonement for the sin of man.

So, back to the point, God will not make us do anything. This is why surrender is the ultimate act of love for God. Once we humble ourselves to a position of surrender, we may come to know truth through Christ. In John 8:32, he shows us through that truth comes spiritual

Please don't carry that old resistance to the term surrender or submission. These are terms of ultimate, sacrificial love as God exhibits them. Before you may know spiritual freedom from your past, you must gain a current understanding of freedom's truth. That truth will only come when you put down your weapons of resistance and give your life to Christ. This act of loving surrender will also help you to maintain your well-earned spiritual freedom.

Soul Ties

We talked about soul ties earlier, but they are so vital to us gaining and maintaining true freedom from our past pain, that I'd like to revisit them while we discuss spiritual freedom.

Soul ties also continue to play a role in your ability to separate yourself from the injuries caused in your past. Whether the past was decades or days ago, you must gain victory over anything that has pierced your spirit to leave a lasting stain.

We get tethered to people, events, reminiscences (true or false), and feelings from our past. There's a difference between memories and soul ties. Memories are recollections of the past that stir a thought. Soul ties are tangible attachments to the past that can create dysfunction in your present.

It's important for your freedom to spend the time to identify these tethers and release yourself from them through confession, forgiveness, and restoration through Christ. New ones develop while old ones may return if we fail to maintain our walk with Christ.

Daily Prayer

Talking about our daily walk with Christ, the best way to pursue that relationship is through daily prayer. Whether it's our wife, kids, friends, or work, little to nothing gets done without communication. How often does God want to connect with us? His word makes it very clear in 1 Thessalonians 5:17.

God wants to share a close relationship with us. I know, it sometimes blows my mind that the creator of everything actually wants to hang out with me.

King David, whom God loved dearly, often struggled with the bigness of God wanting to know him. But the truth is, we were created to glorify Him, and relationships are the best way to do this.

Retrain Your Brain

There are other tactics for making sure you maintain spiritual freedom from your personal past pain. Daily prayer is the foundation that helps you to avoid past habits. I hear it all the time that we cannot control what pops into our mind. I want to assure you that you can. If we look at the brain as an open, unattended back door, then yes, of course sinful thoughts filled with temptation are going to invade your mind and spirit.

God gifted you with an incredible computer, and it's yours to control. What you feed your mind with is what your mind will feed upon. The term, "Thoughts that fire together, wire together," is the perfect description of what happens in the programing of your brain.

I've heard the doubters here too, and I only want to assure you that you do have the authority to retrain your brain. It's called neuroplasticity. I like using this example to explain it.

Let's say you're fighting a porn addiction that began as a result of past pain. I want to reassure you that you have the spiritual ability to end that lust for pornography. To begin with, you were not spiritually created with a thirst for porn. God created us to seek one-on-one relationships with each other. Look to Genesis 2:24 for the creation story of Adam and Eve.

Adam clung to her and they became one flesh. That becoming one flesh includes their spiritual relationship, but also meshing their physical, sexual intimacy into one. It is personal, not anonymous, relationships that we were designed to pursue.

An interesting fact I like to throw in about here is that humans are one of few creatures that mates looking into each other's eyes. This is the core of intimacy, and God reserved that for only us. And, BTW, I'm not suggesting the missionary position is the only option for spouses!

Next, you were not genetically wired to desire watching porn. As a baby, then toddler, child and up until you were first exposed to porn, your brain never sought out sex over cartoons. No, it was an exposure to porn that planted a seed of curiosity or a disturbance that grew into an unhealthy dependence for something to ease your hurts.

Does everyone exposed to porn develop an addiction to it? No, but those who have a spiritual deficit caused by pain are much more prone. Your brain was fed a steady diet of pornography; therefore it developed an appetite for pornography. But, just as your brain desired what it was fed, you can retrain your brain with a steady diet of scripture, prayer, and communication with God.

This doesn't only apply to pornography. We must reprogram our minds against all forms of unhealthy, sin-filled thoughts and actions. We can maintain a safe distance from the past that has plagued us, but it requires us to put away the negative, destructive thinking.

Consider what you watch, read, and discuss each week. The violence, soft porn, and promiscuous relationships on mainstream television provide a steady flow that feeds negativity into your mind and distracts it from God's word. The longer we linger in an unhealthy atmosphere, the further we fall from God.

Look at King David, and we'll see how lingering and filling his mind with lust led to the fall of a mighty man of God. He was on his roof and spotted a woman bathing. That would've been the time to head back into the house where his other six wives were located, but no. The longer David stood lurking, the closer he moved toward sin and the further he fell from God's will.

> *One evening David got up from his bed and walked around on the roof of the palace. From the roof he saw a woman bathing. The woman was very beautiful, and David sent someone to find out about her. The man said, "She is Bathsheba, the daughter of Eliam and the wife of Uriah the Hittite." [4] Then David sent messengers to get her. She came to him, and he slept with her. (Now she was purifying herself from her monthly uncleanness.) Then she went back home. [5] The woman conceived and sent word to David, saying, "I am pregnant."*
> *2 Samuel 11:3-5*

Protect your eyes, ears, and mouth. Don't let the devil lure you to his hook like some trout. There is good in God's word, and in this life, but we must pursue it while we intentionally chose to flee from the allure of sin. Philippians 4:8 explains the things with which God wants us to feed our mind, spirit and soul.

You can do this if you are sincere, purposeful, and expectant. You won't just stumble into a command of your thoughts. It can be done if you are committed to making it happen. Look at what the apostle Paul says about our thoughts. He doesn't say smash them if they pop up in your head like a spiritual game of whack-a-mole. He says take them captive and make them obedient.

The words *take* and *make* are powerful action terms. You make things happen for a living, so be that hero of action by putting these two powerful words into action in your life.

We demolish arguments and every pretension that sets itself up against the knowledge of God, and we take captive every thought to make it obedient to Christ.
2 Corinthians 10:5

Call To Action

1. Write out a recurring negative thought in detail.
2. Write out why you think that thought is so dominant in your mind.
3. Write out a creative, imaginative description of a jailer taking that negative thought as a prisoner and subjecting it to the spiritual justice system.
4. Write out three positive memories in detail.

9

INNER VOWS

Therefore, my friends, I want you to know that through Jesus the forgiveness of sins is proclaimed to you. ³⁹ Through Him everyone who believes is set free from every sin, a justification you were not able to obtain under the law of Moses.
Acts 13:38-39

* * *

Inner vows are common among most people. We make them as kids, teens, and young adults. They range from what we'll be when we grow up, to who we'll marry, to what type of job we'll secure.

While these can be harmless aspirations and life goals, the critical point is that they can become destructive because of the emotional framework being erected outside of God's will for our life.

Let's take a quick step back and define just what an inner vow is so we're on the same page. According to Pastor Jimmy Evans, from his book *Freedom From Your Past*, they are a self-oriented commitment made in response to a person, experience, or desire in life.

I was fifteen years old, and a brand-new licensed driver. Of course that meant I volunteered to take the old wood-grain paneled station wagon everywhere. As I sat in a fast-food restaurant waiting for my younger brother to return, a man I never knew came up to my open window.

I was a good-sized athlete, but I was still fifteen years old. The man began to berate me and taunt me until I was reaching for the door handle. That's when the pistol slipped through the window and pressed smack against my temple. It was a small town. It was 1980, and people didn't do things like that to kids, right?

I was immediately so afraid, and then suddenly I was not. I didn't even know what he was saying after I felt the metal barrel against my skin. All I wanted to do was kill him for making me feel afraid. I swore I'd find him, and I'd make him pay for what he did to me that day. Every time I drove that old wagon through town, I looked for him. I didn't know if it was out of fear or an actual desire to kill him, but revenge was my inner vow.

It was a big part of why I wanted to enter law enforcement. I never wanted to be afraid again. I also wanted to stop people from threatening others. In a way, I spent over twenty-five years taking out my revenge on those people who preyed upon others. Did that inner vow lead to something good? In a way it led me into policing, but the destructive nature of it caused an obsession to flee from fear while always bent on exacting revenge.

When we are hurt as a child or younger person, it's not uncommon to respond emotionally in anger with an inner vow to curse something or avoid the source of that pain. If we were whipped by a parent, and it embarrassed us, then it would be an expected response as a child to vow to never whip or discipline our own kids. While that might sound like a noble gesture at the time, the reality is that as a parent who refuses to discipline will produce unruly kids without structure.

Not to mention, your spouse who may grow frustrated by your refusal to take charge of the kids. Beyond their displeasure at your failing to parent the children, and the bad uncorrected behavior of the kids, your spouse's dissatisfaction stems from not understanding why you refuse to correct your very own children.

The truth is, you probably don't remember making that inner vow as a young child while on the receiving end of a switch or belt. But, the reality is, once you make these self-directed statements, you have the potential for igniting a pattern of dysfunction and misery.

Other common inner vows are:

- I'll never let anyone hurt me again.
- I'll never be poor like my parents.
- I'll never trust anyone again.
- I'll give my own kids everything they want.
- I'll never let my wife talk to me that way.
- I'll never wait on God to do something I want now.

Do these sound familiar? I'll give you a chance to write out your own in a bit, but for now, think through the times you may have purposefully or inadvertently made inner vows out of embarrassment, anger, or frustration. The danger is with the self-oriented intention.

Anything directed inward, as opposed to outward to God, eliminates God from the process, and most importantly the outcome. Is accumulating wealth bad? No, God wants to bless us in all things, but when the accumulation was made as a result of an inner vow, then God was not part of the process. This opens the door for money to become your god (lower case g).

Because you were embarrassed by being poor as a child, you now find yourself outside of God's will and blessings just so you could show Him and your family that you are in control of wealth accumulation. That's a dangerous and painful place to be.

Because we are focusing on freeing ourselves from past personal pain, inner vows not only imprint a pattern of self-reliance, but from the moment of that vow, we're tethered to that past event. The irony is that whatever you promised to escape, flee from, or avoid earlier in life, will continue to haunt you because you're chained to it via the inner vow.

Remember when we talked about soul ties? This is right there with shackles to the past. They can and must be broken in order to move forward and be free from the effects of pain.

Three of the most dangerous aspects of inner vows are:

1. They are unscriptural:

God says do not swear at all (Matthew 5:33-37) because inner vows do not submit itself to God. Jesus says, "perform your oaths to the Lord..." but with inner vows, there is no obligation or submission to God. Everything done and accomplished is done internally for self-gratification.

2. They have an unseen effect:

As we discussed earlier, you may not even realize that you locked your future self into a pattern of behavior outside of God's will. And while it may take years or even decades before you understand what is going down, it eventually comes to a head for conflict.

This is called the "sleeper" effect, and results from a vow lying dormant until triggered by an action or response. When examined through God goggles, you see how much hurt has been suffered by you and caused to others by you. Inner vows create this pain environment because you're in charge and God isn't.

3. They are the most powerful form of commitment:

Inner vows are powerful because they were made by you, and at a time of hurt or turmoil that affected you. Because you personally removed God from the equation, you have a tendency to cling to the vow no matter what the cost to you or others.

Pain, anger and desperation make for a lethal combination. You will not know inner peace until you have freed yourself from the consequences of selfish inner vows. They are a curse and judgment upon the situation you were in because of your sorrow. God is very clear that if we judge others, He will judge us just as harshly.

How to Unlock Inner Vows

The first step to breaking free from the shackles of an inner vow is to identify the vow itself. I know it's impossible to retrace every thought or word spoken over the course of your life. But if you begin by looking back on times that your parents failed you, or at least at the time you thought they failed you, that is a great start.

Next, process through negative events, thoughts, and actions related to life moments. Were there times where you passed strong judgments about your parents, or your past, or about your ideals for your future?

I'll share one from my childhood, and although it seemed innocent, as I matured, it caused grief for me and my family. There were seven of us kids in my family. My parents rushed us everywhere from ball practice to the grocery store as best they could with one car.

The result was a few times arriving late to practice or an event, but oddly enough never late for school. It drove me nuts, and I would complain from the time we left until they dropped me off. I swore I'd never be late once I was able to drive. I was angry at them for making me miss moments of whatever we were going to because it embarrassed me to be late.

For decades, that inner vow caused an obsession with punctuality. Now before you say, that's a good thing, did you catch that I said an "obsession"? That not only went for me, but anyone who worked for me, my wife, kids, friends, people in the drive-thru, airlines, etc.

I timed everything. As the commander of a large multi-jurisdictional drug task force, I would even get aggravated at the dealers who we'd set up undercover drug purchases from. If we agreed to meet at a place for seven p.m., then I expected them to be there at seven p.m. Of course, drug dealers and criminals use their own system of timekeeping—none.

There were more than a few drug deals called off during surveillance because the crooks were late. I guess in my obsession with punctuality, they either needed to learn to be on time, or do without getting busted and going to prison.

At the source, it was more about a selfish boy not wanting to miss a single pitch or be embarrassed by sprinting across the field after everyone else had arrived. I also placed harsh judgment against my parents, although they hustled more than anyone, I knew just so we wouldn't have to miss out on being involved.

While I obsessed over time, I didn't waste any time in rebuking that inner vow and praying freedom and restoration over it. I was amazed, once freed, at how much stress it used to cause in my daily life. Yeah and everyone else's too.

Once I came to understand the destructive nature of my punctuality obsession, I took off the only watch I'd worn throughout most of my law enforcement career. It meant so much to me because we'd been through countless tough times together. I left it in the city I was visiting when I freed myself from the curse of that childhood inner vow. Freedom for me required a physical act to show my discipline and appreciation for God's grace. Now, I don't expect you to leave watches all over the country, but the idea is to put grace into action and make real-life, tangible changes.

Inner vows are connected to the level of strong judgments and unforgiveness against people in your life. To break free and liberate yourself from the past pains that prompted the vows, you must identify them, confess them, repent, and pray for God's restoration.

Call To Action

1. Write out in detail what you understand to be your inner vows.
2. Write out in detail what you remember as the cause for having prompted you to make the inner vows.
3. Write out periods in your life when you have condemned others with strong judgments that have led to making inner vows.
4. Write out in detail one example of an inner vow and how it affects you today.

10

JUDGMENTS

But now that you have been set free from sin and have become slaves of God, the benefit you reap leads to holiness, and the result is eternal life.
Romans 6:22

* * *

"He's a squirrel."

Those were words I'd endure over years from a fellow agent. His favorite pastime was casting judgments on others. What he meant by being a squirrel bounced around from being other than white to being late for lunch. The guy was toxic, and in the end, guess who was the squirrel? I think we all work with these guys at some point or another. They hate themselves and everyone so much that despite your efforts to mentor or correct their behavior, they've appointed themselves judge, jury, and social executioner.

This is an important section to discuss because God's word covers judgment all throughout the bible. The effects of passing judgment are rooted in spiritual laws and consequences. I'm sure as you're reading this, your mind has already wandered off to "Judge not, lest ye be judged." Yeah, so has mine.

This is how vital it is to understand the connection between judging and past pain. Without even knowing where that line from the bible is located, it's indelibly embedded in our brains. It's Matthew 7:1, by the way, but I'll share more of that and other key scripture showing you both sides of the blessing or curse that we rain down upon ourselves with judgments.

Now, let's be honest in making judgment about others. I'm guilty of it, and although I really try to avoid casting judgment, I still catch myself doing it. When we do this, it's similar to placing a curse in action. Except that according to God's word, we reap what we sow, as well as we are judged by the same measure that we have judged.

As first responders and dealing with the public daily, it's important to avoid the trap of judgment. Not only can it impair a bias against people we swore to serve, but that judgment harms your own spirit as a reflection of stepping away from God's will. Be aware of the connection of judgment and past pain. They feed off of each other.

We live under two very certain and undeniable sets of laws . The spiritual laws reveal God's character, and the physical laws govern the world we live in. When we judge others, we set the spiritual laws into effect, and while we may not recognize this, they are still very much in action.

The laws of judgments attach us to past pain, and they must be dealt with according to scripture. But first, check out this proof for your authorization as found in God's word: Romans 2:1; Luke 6:37 and Matthew 7:1-2.

When we judge someone, we are assessing a value, usually a diminished value on that person. Yet who are we to judge anyone? This is where the violation occurs, and it is not without consequence. God is our king and our judge, so when we do it, we not only remove Him from our life, but we take His place.

In the three scripture verses above, we see that by judging another:

1. We are condemned,
2. We are ourselves judged, and,
3. We are judged by the same measure or standard we used against the other person.

It's so important for first responders to understand how serious this is. We operate in a world where we make assessments on a daily basis. Many times, those involve life or death scenarios, and always, they affect other people. Even if it's just a small structural fire that's extinguished, someone had to respond and someone owns the property that is now in need of repair.

Getting trapped into the habit of ramping up decisions and assessments to the level of judgments is dangerous. I know I've made my share of side-handed comments about people who were less than helpful. We walk a fine line, but clearly defining the differences will help you make sure not to cross over to the risk of judgments.

As a kid, I loved to fight, mock, and tease all of my siblings, no matter how much older some were. My mother warned me against making ugly faces at them and said one day that an ugly face would stick. Although she didn't realize it, she was right on the mark about violating God's law of judgments. The ugly nature we show others is what we will be shown.

The seeds we sow in our youth or earlier adulthood will always come back to be reaped. It might be an immediate response or lie dormant for decades before rearing its vicious head. But you can be sure that who and what you condemn will become you and what you despise most.

We've covered, and will continue to examine, the effects of past personal pain and its effects on us today. So much of the pain we carry is a result of our childhood and earlier life. Sometimes that pain results from injury or physical abuse, while other times it occurs when abandoned or neglected. In all of these main instances, pain results from our being a victim. And as an emergency first responder, we do not like being the victim.

In the incident of judgment, just as in the case of making inner vows, we are the instigator. A firefighter I never met personally, but we'll call Troy, asked me to mentor him through text and social media. Troy confessed he struggled with alcoholism. Of course, his drinking led to him being demoted and fired from one jurisdiction before landing a job in a much smaller town. His drinking also led to his first divorce. He was deep into the process for his second failed marriage and wanted desperately to save it.

He was upfront about the abuse of alcohol to cover feeling bad about himself. He'd thought about suicide, but he said that he believed in God and was afraid of the consequences. To me, that was a great sign that Troy was in it to win it, but he just didn't have the tools to bring home the victory.

We began to discuss his past, and not surprisingly, he had major conflicts with his dad. His father was a hard worker who hit the bottle as soon as he hit the front door.

While neither Troy nor his mom were physically abused when his dad was drunk, they were neglected. His dad's drinking led to physical ailments and loss of work, and then poverty for the family before he walked away from Troy and his mom.

Troy hated his dad for what he'd done to his mom and him. He swore he'd never drink a drop of alcohol and cursed his dad because of it. Troy's bitter judgment of his father, who as a child was horribly abused by his own alcoholic father (Troy's grandfather), caused Troy to become the object that his judgment hated—a divorced alcoholic.

We worked backward through his past until he was able to identify not only soul ties, but the inner vow based on a condemning judgment against his father. Troy worked to confess his sin, repent, and pray for God's restoration with his wife.

Sowing and Reaping

Troy was fortunate to have plugged into God's spiritual laws before he again found himself divorced. It was through God's forgiving grace that Troy saved himself and his marriage by shattering shackles from his past. His violation was also an example of moving beyond the law of judgment and into the spiritual realm of sowing and reaping. Both are closely connected.

Do not be deceived: God cannot be mocked. A man reaps what he sows. [8] *Whoever sows to please their flesh, from the flesh will reap destruction; whoever sows to please the Spirit, from the Spirit will reap eternal life.* [9] *Let us not become weary in doing good, for at the proper time we will reap a harvest if we do not give up.*
Galatians 6:7-9

Solid principles of sowing and reaping:

1. Whatever you sow, will come back to you.
2. Whatever you sow, will multiply upon return.
3. Whatever you sow, will be reaped in its own time.
4. Whatever you sow, will return in like fashion. Good cannot come from bad, nor will bad come from good seed (Luke 6:43-44).

There is spiritual authority in our words. Our tongue has the power of life and death, so if you sincerely want to gain freedom from your past, please weigh your words wisely. Especially regarding harsh judgments of other people. Speak truth to power and life-giving encouragement to others, and you shall receive blessings of like kind.

Call To Action

1. Write out in detail condemning words of judgment that you commonly speak.
2. Write out in detail three judgments against people in your past.
3. Write out whether what you judged these people for has yet to carry over to characteristics you know you exhibit.
4. Write out a prayer confessing your judgment, request for forgiveness, and your blessings for those you harmed.

11

PTSD AND SOUL SCARS

For the creation was subjected to frustration, not by its own choice, but by the will of the one who subjected it, in hope [21] that the creation itself will be liberated from its bondage to decay and brought into the freedom and glory of the children of God.
Romans 8:20-21

* * *

Injuries cause scars that serve as a reminder of past pain. Unlike physical restoration, emotional, mental and spiritual injuries don't naturally heal over time. While the body launches into an immediate recovery phase after experiencing a physical wound, your spirit remains vulnerable. As a matter of fact, those injuries get more severe the longer left unattended.

Time does not heal all wounds.

My wife and I were talking about parents and pain one afternoon. So much of our dysfunction can be linked directly to things they did or didn't do during our childhood. I remarked that it was almost impossible to be a parent and not mess up your kids.

. . .

The truth is, no one is perfect. Through our lives we will hurt and be hurt. The difference for parents who believe in Jesus Christ is that they've placed Him as the head of their marriage and children. Following Christ's example helps parents minimize the damage or recognize it when done and work to restore the child.

Left undone, it's easy for us as first responders to carry that pain into our high-stress jobs. We either block out all empathy for ourselves and our victims, or we flood each case assignment with an internal desire to make every wrong right in the victims' lives. This is especially dangerous because we tend to wear it on our sleeves without processing the harm done by others' trauma.

Without the tools to process our trauma, and the secondary trauma of others, we enter the danger zone for cumulative PTSD. There's a gap in knowledge within the first responder community where PTSD is considered. The most well-defined awareness is for military service members returning home after experiencing combat-related post-traumatic stress. This is usually the result of one or a few incidents of truly horrific experiences.

First responders, as research has shown, are susceptible not only to the isolated incidents, but also as an effect of cumulative PTSD. This form is often more dangerous because it usually goes undiagnosed. Unlike the tragic incident such as an officer-involved shooting that can be pinpointed, the daily grind that leads to the cumulative effect isn't realized until we're deep in over our head.

The damages of PTSD are exponentially increased when compounded by unhealed soul scars from past pain. It's often the exposure to past pain that opens the door to the cumulative effects taking a tighter hold as opposed to someone else without the history of hurting.

Contrary to the limited exposure to trauma, cumulative PTSD may result from exposure to high-threat calls for service like barricaded suspects, hostage standoffs, felony drug busts, fatal car crashes, and responding to calls where someone has been seriously injured or killed.

I'll never un-live my first or final death on duty. It's not something we're conditioned to deal with, yet in between speeding cars and school zones, come the dead and dying. My first duty death experience was a call where I administered CPR to a retired cop who was dying. I worked like a madman alternating between breaths and compressions. He died. I was devastated and felt responsible. I never told a soul, and yet I never forgot the night I mistook the air I compressed out of his lungs for having saved his life.

My last on-duty death was a two-year-old girl who ran from her mother's grip in a shopping center parking lot. A full-sized pickup truck hit her, and its front driver's tire rolled over and crushed the little girl's skull. There was nothing the driver could've done. And there was absolutely nothing I could do. After almost twenty-six years on the job, I felt just as helpless as that rookie cop decades earlier.

But as you well know, it's not always the horrible calls for service that dump the most stress on us. Often, it's the difficult hours and shift work, overtime, being called in on days off for court, training, or case follow-ups. The anticipation of what and when the next call might be. I've patrolled eleven hours before catching a radio call. It was like jumping into a full-out spring after just waking up from a nap.

Simply having to deal with other people's negative attitudes and knowing that one slip of your tongue in setting them straight or taking up for yourself could see you before an internal affairs investigation. I've often said it was more dangerous in the office than out on the streets because of the internal politics and backstabbing among the brethren.

Signs of PTSD

Early identification is vital for getting the proper diagnosis and treatment in overcoming PTSD. Too many of us say we'll get help later, but later may be too late.

I had loved ones beg me to get help. I even knew the early signs, but worried that seeking help would be the kiss of death. Besides, I worked twelve years of undercover and sixteen years in SWAT, and we did not show weakness. I used to joke that once I retired, I'd find help. It took about a solid year of counseling to free me of the demons of post-traumatic stress. That was also about the time I unloaded Mr. "In Case Of."

Being a hero is great. Being a stubborn hard-ass is just selfish and dangerous. Seek help sooner rather than later. Here are physical signs:

- Fatigue
- Vomiting or nausea
- Chest pain
- Twitches
- Thirst
- Insomnia or nightmares
- Breathing difficulty
- Grinding of teeth
- Profuse sweating
- Pounding heart
- Diarrhea or intestinal upsets
- Headaches

In addition to the physical signs that may alert you to the symptoms of PTSD, here are a few behavioral triggers that should alert you:

- Withdrawal from family and friends
- Pacing and restlessness
- Emotional outbursts
- Antisocial acts
- Suspicion and paranoia
- Increased alcohol consumption and other substance abuse

And finally, there will be emotional signs to help clue you into the reality that there is a problem:

- Anxiety or panic
- Guilt
- Fear
- Denial
- Irritability
- Depression
- Intense anger
- Agitation
- Apprehension

PTSD has become almost chic among the alpha crowd. It gets blamed and credited for either too much or not enough damage in an officer's life. It's rooted in pain that can ruin a career and drive us to take our life. The truth to remember is the scars on our spirit will not heal until we allow them to be healed.

The first time my pastor said that to me, I was stunned. I thought who in the world would not want to allow themselves to be healed? Honestly, I was unknowingly one of them. There are several reasons, but intimidation and being ridiculed by others are the top two.

If you'll recall earlier, I shared an experience of investigating a serial child molester. Although we'd identified and contacted victims going back over twenty years, none of the men would admit they were molested by the man while they were kids. Sure, these men were victims and they needed help in the worst way, but they'd rather exist in their fractured husks than reclaim victory through Christ.

I don't, and never would, condemn the victims. It was their choice, and although I grieved for each one's loss of childhood innocence, I understood the personal choices each made. The point I want to share is that there are many reasons first responders don't seek healing, and these are just two.

You'd also be surprised to know that in this world of everything online, many of us don't know where to get the help to heal. Where do we begin? Since most of us want to avoid the risk of public exposure, asking others for help or a reference limits potential resources right off the bat.

I will share that there are several levels of care that you may need depending on how deep your injuries go. But because there is a spiritual connection between cause and cure, I always suggest that first responders seek out the counsel of their pastor. Many faith leaders are trained and focus their ministry on healing the hurts that harm our walk with Christ.

If you have a pastor, please go speak with him. If it is a situation requiring another level of care, they will refer you. Don't feel as though you are being passed around. Each situation is different and may require care ranging from conversation to medication. But you'll never know unless you're willing to trust someone to get started in the healing process.

If you are suffering and don't think you can trust opening up to someone, then you're experiencing yet another reason why we first responders remained trapped in pain—*denial*.

I know how important silence and isolationism is to our culture. We rarely trust anyone who doesn't serve, but this is a spiritual realm where the only way to get help is to open up so you can be helped. Keep shoptalk inside the circle but find someone to share your pain.

First responders will go to just about any length to avoid something we have zero interest or understanding in. One of the most common ways we do this is by suppressing emotions about the event. We can't hurt because we're warriors. Right? The best way to avoid the pain is to avoid the feelings associated with it. That's like saying if I avoid the blood running out of my chest, then the bullet that's in there will go away.

Disassociation is a tactic we use to distance ourselves from the act that hurt us. But even if the distance is physical space, the tether that ties you to it is always right around the corner. Besides, you can't selectively shut off one emotion without adversely affecting other emotions.

Besides destructive behavior such as defensiveness, external influencers like drugs and alcohol exponentially increase the risk and damage caused by the pain. Bigger problems arise once our focus is now placed on fighting addictions, as opposed to healing the wounds that caused the pain requiring us to "medicate" ourselves.

Like most things in life, there is a process involved. Just in case you are curious why God doesn't snap His fingers and make your pain go away, it's important to understand the different types of healing.

1. Instant healing by miracle:

There are countless examples of immediate healings performed by God or God through Jesus. They were quick and seemed effortless on behalf of Jesus.

Despite the various ailments, the common factor, besides Jesus, was that those healed believed in the power to be healed. They were miracles and occurred not because of how good or bad the person was, but because that was the process by which God chose to heal them.

2. Healing by process:

Whether healing is instant or occurs over a long period of time, it is the process for restoration. God may speed it up, or slow it down, but never forget that God sets the pace and the degree of restoration. What is important is that God's word promises the end result, not how long it takes.

How often have we passed through a trial, and once it's over, we've either forgotten what we'd been through, or come to understand changes in our lives as a result of having gone through something? Part of God's healing process is education.

Remember when Lazarus's family begged Jesus to run to him? What did Jesus do? He took four days before He arrived at the tomb of His friend. Lazarus had even begun to rot, and his flesh stunk, but Jesus was in no hurry. Why wasn't He?

There was a process. There were people besides Lazarus who would benefit in faith through this process, and while the end result was imminent, the process vetted out doubts, fears, and hope from those attached to the process. Read John 11:1-46 for yourself and mark down how many people close to Christ behaved less than faithfully.

Just as in the example of Lazarus being raised from the dead, there were feelings present during the process of healing. No matter how hard first responders try to pretend we don't have feelings, the truth is *we do*. It doesn't mean we have to weep at the coffee shop or during shift change, but the process of healing from past personal pain involves our being able to understand why we feel the way we do.

1. Anger

Denial bottles up lots of emotion. It doesn't naturally process, so we have to find outlets. Once we open up to the process of healing, we'll see that anger has been waiting to rage for a while.

. . .

This anger also has two options—to manifest internally or externally. Usually anger is directed at whomever it was that hurt you. If it was your dad, then you may seek out revenge, but please understand the consequences. Restoration is a much better option.

Instead of seeking out spiritual restoration with the one who caused your pain, some first responders attack themselves through shame, guilt, or depression for allowing themselves to have been victimized. Please don't measure your adult expectations by the child's reactions.

Remember in either outlet, you are not responsible for what was done to you then, but you are responsible for how you handle it now. Also, since we're giving good one-liner advice, anger is not a sin, as long as you don't sin in your anger.

> *"Be angry, and do not sin":*
> *do not let the sun go down on your wrath,*
> *Ephesians 4:26*

Since we're talking about anger, and I shared one of my favorite sayings about anger not being a sin as long as we don't sin in anger, I want to touch a pressure point about our fraternity. It is wrapped up in anger, pain, and shame. It's a desperate, dangerous cry for control because through our pain, we feel as though we've lost control.

Domestic violence committed by law enforcement, in particular, is experienced in at least 40% of police families as opposed to 10% of families in the general public. Experienced officers expose their families to domestic violence four times more often than other families. The truth you know as well as I do is that these studies are so underreported because of our practice of handling things in-house.

If you are endangering your family because of your behavior, please don't blame it on the spouse, the job stress, or the dog. It's yours, so own it. You need help immediately because it's an escalating pattern often leading to murder-suicide. You're not mad at your spouse, you're angry at your past. Allow yourself to heal.

2. Grieving

Similar to the stages of death and loss, we must process our emotions. Unlike death, where there is either no notice or a relatively contained period before the loss, the emotional upheaval we'll have to face has been buried just below our spirit's surface since the injury.

Grieving is important for allowing a balance to anger. It usually begins as the process of anger is resolved or managed. You may feel as though these days are your darkest and you can't hold on any longer but let me assure you that healing is yours.

I've lost seven friends to line-of-duty deaths during my years in law enforcement. All were personal friends, and while I still miss each one dearly, I was able to grieve their passing to move forward and through the pain. Except one.

Since I won't name the others, I'll refer to him by his nickname, Ox. We were friends before we both entered law enforcement. He was my best friend, and even stood in my wedding in 1989. We worked undercover narcotics and SWAT until he moved to a new agency. He was murdered on June 16, 2006, and a massive manhunt ensued before his killer was captured.

I was my nationally accredited agency's SWAT commander and requested activation to assist in the search across parish (county) lines. A spiteful supervisor denied the request. The anger I felt prevented the grieving I needed. Carrying the grudge of unforgiveness lasted about two years before I came to understand that all I was doing was hurting myself by not allowing the grieving process to move forward.

The truth is, there are crummy people in our profession. They will do things on purpose to hurt us. This causes so much stress and expands the open borders of pain we already harbor.

Broken and Blue

Forgiveness is vital to not only liberating ourselves from them, but also giving ourselves the space to grieve.

This is the season Jesus has been waiting for. He sincerely wants to help you, but He will not force Himself into a situation where He is not welcomed. This is the blessing of free will once again.

Christ has been waiting on you (Revelation 3:20), but the denial, anger, disassociation, and every layer of separation you placed between yourself and the reality of what harmed you has created a barrier. Now is the time to tear that wall down between you and the healing grace of Jesus Christ.

3. Acceptance

Rarely are we harmed by strangers. What makes the hurt so much more intense is the loss of innocence and trust from the known person. There was an expected honor code of adult protector that was violated when the protector became the violator.

That violation not only left soul scars because of what action was perpetrated, but the trust was broken. The physical body can heal itself or be healed. Soul scars are very different, and responses to violations of trust hurt deeper than broken bones or bruises.

Once we have processed our healing and as part of that, been able to forgive and bless those who hurt us, a spirit of acceptance gives us peace. It is not a feeling of joy or happiness, but it is a long-gone contentment over what had once hurt you having been processed and placed in the past so you may move forward in the life God created you to enjoy.

I guess in a way, I needed to reach a point of acceptance after I retired from policing. I had so many big plans. I was no longer shackled to a job where an unrelenting and over-demanding public beckoned for my attention. It was time to soar. That first year was a bust.

. . .

Although it was my decision to retire, I still had lingering hurt from the only job I'd known my entire adult life. It took time to decompress and process what had actually caused me pain, versus what were painful memories. I have reached a point of contentment and have no regrets for my service or my retirement.

Call To Action

1. Write out what you picture your soul scars to be.
2. Write out a list of who caused soul scars upon your spirit.
3. Write out a list of who on the previous list has yet to be forgiven by you.
4. Looking back at the symptoms list for PTSD, write out in detail which of those you have you had or currently experience.
5. Write out in detail how you have compensated in ways to avoid having to deal with the pain.
6. Write out a prayer for your coming to heal completely.

12

UNSEEN ENEMIES

Therefore, there is now no condemnation for those who are in Christ Jesus, [2] because through Christ Jesus the law of the Spirit who gives life has set you free from the law of sin and death. [3] For what the law was powerless to do because it was weakened by the flesh, God did by sending His own Son in the likeness of sinful flesh to be a sin offering. And so He condemned sin in the flesh, [4] in order that the righteous requirement of the law might be fully met in us, who do not live according to the flesh but according to the Spirit.
Romans 8:1-4

* * *

I truly appreciate you sticking with me throughout this. I've prayed over our work and the effort we're putting into it. I know it's challenging to dig deep but regaining your freedom from a life of past pain is worth the work. It has changed my life from one of suffering in the darkness of addiction, shame, and guilt, to living victorious in Christ.

. . .

77

These next two chapters involve some heavy stuff, and as much as I was tempted to gloss over them, the reality is if we're in the battle for freedom, then we need to know as much about the enemy as they know about us.

When I tell people that it was safer to work undercover than being assigned to uniformed patrol, they think I'm kidding. They can't even begin to imagine that a DEA drug sting is less risky than a traffic stop. It was a matter of risk mitigation.

Risk was reduced because we didn't just focus on some random dealer. Our targets were researched, surveilled, and infiltrated with informants or wiretaps. Simply put, we knew the violator better than they knew themselves. I was an expert at knowing the seen enemy.

As I came to understand, we also have enemies in an unseen realm. I was challenged to fully recognize what that meant and how they posed threats to us. These enemies can cause us to stumble if we don't commit the time to learn about them. If unexposed, they'll cause more damage than a parking lot ambush.

We all have those people out there who, for whatever reason, do not like us or have a penchant for causing grief. But here I'm talking about the spiritual realm and satanic forces. This is also where some first responders either flip to the next chapter or balk at the progress they've made so far and check out. Don't do it—stick together.

The devil does exist and is wholly invested in separating us from God. My pastor helped me understand the battle that has raged for thousands of years, but in the beginning, I was unsure of what I was being told or what it had to do with my position as chief of police. He would tell me that my battle wasn't against crime in the city; it was a supernatural war between good and evil (Ephesians 6:12). To be honest, it freaked me out a bit at first, and if I had my choice at that moment, I would've stuck to fighting bad guys.

. . .

Broken and Blue

Over the years, I saw what he referred to, as he continued to pray over me to sustain me in that fight. I'll share a few things I learned during my immersion experience as the head of an agency tasked with leading and protecting others.

1. The supernatural realm is very real.
2. This is not a battle we can win on our own.
3. The war has already been won with the crucifixion and resurrection of Jesus Christ.
4. The attacks are relentless, but God has given us His armor of protection.
5. Satan uses anyone and everyone against you. Even yourself.
6. Through faith we have the authority to resist the devil and he will flee.
7. Satan is not God, so he is not omnipresent, but he has legions of demons at his command.
8. There is no neutral ground in this war. You are either under the grace of God or the control of Satan.

The pain, shame, and guilt you've carried with you is a result of the devil's consistent campaign to keep you separated from God. That's his entire purpose, because once he's got you on your own, you're easy prey. The devil specializes in the world of steal, kill, and destroy. Once you are divided from God, you'll soon find yourself apart from your wife, kids, life, and faith. Everything that is important to you becomes a target for this lethal sharpshooter.

You see, the devil can only destroy because he's never created anything. Remember as a kid, you'd build a fantastic something or another with your Lincoln Logs or Legos, only to turn around to see a kid brother knocking it down while laughing like a hyena? That's the devil. No, your brother isn't the devil, or maybe he is, but it's the same thing Satan specializes in—destruction.

. . .

Even the devil's name is rooted in division. *Dia-bolos* in Greek means, "the one who divides." Ever watched those wildlife shows? The predator rushes into the pack to divide them. They spot the weaker animals, so they launch toward them again. The flock divides into an even smaller group. Finally, you may see the vulnerable one with one other animal, usually the mother of the intended victim. But, skilled as the animal is, the last approach divides them and leaves the target alone and defenseless. That's you without Christ.

We just talked about the need for Christ to begin healing the soul scars from our past. It's impossible without Him. This is why it's so crucial for Satan to divide us from God, so that we remain in our pain and sin. In that state, there is no healing, only continued suffering because he's pushed the "shut up" button so we'd fear exposure from peers.

While we're better off focusing on the miraculous authority of God's dominion over this world than Satan's efforts to destroy it, I wanted to give a few scriptural references to verify the demonic presence on this earth. It's really too bad people, even believers, have minimized Satan into a rogue with horns and a pointy tail. He is much more than a cartoon. As a matter of tactic, when Satan shows up, he appears as everything you ever thought you wanted.

Be alert and of sober mind. Your enemy the devil prowls around like a roaring lion looking for someone to devour.
1 Peter 5:8

In Revelation, Jesus states very clearly that the devil, and a third of the angels who followed him, were not only cast out of heaven, but specifically thrown to earth.

The great dragon was hurled down—that ancient serpent called the devil, or Satan, who leads the whole world astray. He was hurled to the earth, and his angels with him.
Revelation 12:9

Since the devil made his first appearance in the Garden of Eden, he's been on the prowl for you and me. There are four primary tactics used by the devil to interfere in our walk with Christ.

1. **Deception** – This is his master skill set. He manipulates us into thinking we're beyond broken and unworthy of healing repair. Satan leads us to believe God doesn't love us, so we never deserve to be healed. He's the father of lies, so anything negative that stops you from breaking free from past personal pain is the work of the devil.

After my second divorce, I realized that I had to stop using wedding rings to search for the love and affirmation I never received from my parents. Instead, I entered into a long-term sexual relationship. Stupidly, I assumed that it was the healthier route, and there were no obligations to worry about. Unfortunately, this woman had other ideas. Despite agreeing to the no commitment or expectation agreement, she desired, what else, a wedding ring.

She was a master at deception and manipulation. While I focused on my career, she focused on keeping me tethered to her no matter what it took. I was blinded by her tactics because selfishly, I was able to commit my time to work, have sex when I wanted it, and go on living the life I thought was productive.

What was actually demonic deception was what I naively dismissed as female drama. Since I was living a life of sin, there was no spiritual discernment thanks to my separation from God's grace. I allowed myself to be led into remaining attached to her because of the negative ideations she bombarded me with. There are consequences for sin, and to think there are no obligations when we engage in illegitimate behavior is personal and professional suicide.

2. Occult Activity – God warned us about witchcraft, but for some rebellious reason, His people have been vulnerable to activities, music, movies, rituals, and anything Satan deceives them into believing holds special power. God holds the power, not tricks and charms.

I grew up in an area of south Louisiana dominated by the Catholic religion with a heavy blending of Creole voodoo and Santeria. I regularly responded to crimes where evidence of the occult was present. As a result, I learned to sense the demonic presence over the entirety of a geographic region. While there are many people living within that realm, those who are under the protection of God are immune or oblivious to the detrimental effects. But, because I was able to witness the effects it had on people and the crimes they committed, it left an indelible impression of the real-world, demonic presence and practice of the occult.

3. Physical Illness – While Satan is not a god, he does rule over a kingdom. Within his kingdom are legions of demons at various ranks like any established army. Demonic possession is real, and God's word gives us numerous examples of physical healings once spirits were cast out.

I know we've all witnessed or know of situations where only by the grace of God was someone healed from the incurable. The area I grew up in was called cancer alley. I believe that the connection to geographic demonic influence and the higher-than-normal incidents of cancer diagnosis are related. Of course, I've seen healings where medical professionals can only attribute the cure to Christ.

4. Mental Disorders – Not every form of mental disorder is demonic, but beyond health defects, many are. Even the effects of low self-esteem, fear, shame, insecurity, and depression can be linked to the devil's lies and division. He causes doubt, which leads to separation from God.

An agency I worked for was a large, nationally accredited sheriff's office. One of our most productive sections was called police social services. They responded to victims needs, enforcing protective orders and obtaining coroner's hold for psychological evaluations. Working closely with this section, I was able to witness first the extreme incidents of mental disorders non-diagnosable by any other explanation than demonic suppression.

Let's wrap this up with the good news of Jesus Christ. A very big part of His ministry's emphasis was on healing and deliverance. Jesus cast out demons to restore health and stability. He still heals, and He will heal you by setting you free from the bonds of your past pain. But you must allow Him in.

Spiritual Oppression

The last section about unseen enemies was hard to write. It became an effort as my distraction level caused several days of delay. The Holy Spirit was definitely in my corner as I pushed through doubts and worries about how you might perceive so much focus on the reality of demonic interference in our lives. But, in typical Holy Spirit fashion, there was no option other than presenting the truth.

I know we first responders can get uncomfortable talking about the spiritual realm. It's outside of things we can grab on to and rattle or finesse until fixed. But it plays a huge role in our lives of past personal pain.

While not biblical, I thought about Sun Tzu's quote, and I paraphrase, "Know thy enemy, know thyself." This is true for those of us who are struggling against something beyond themselves, a family member, co-worker, or others.

Let's not play games here; the enemy is the devil, and he is out to kill, steal, and destroy. God's word describes him as a lion looking to devour us. So, it's important to know the enemy. Actually, our lives depend upon it.

I'll confess that the reality of a demonic spirit fighting for space in my life can be a bit intimidating, but that is the truth, and if you believe in God, Jesus, and the Holy Spirit, then you must accept that demons do exist. God says so.

A common concern about demonic possession is how it affects your life and whether people can actually be possessed. I know most people imagine Linda Blair in *The Exorcist*, but this is real life and a real concern. Discussing the demonic realm is also what stops some of us from reaching the truth because there's a fear that if we mention it, it might target us.

Lack of knowledge creates a boogeyman concept of a very real part of our lives. To answer the question about possession, a Christian cannot be possessed by the devil or a demonic spirit. We were bought by and belong to God. He doesn't trade us off like a used squad car for a newer cruiser.

Nonbelievers are a different story. I'd mentioned it before and it's worth another reminder that if you don't believe and belong to God, then you serve Satan. There is no neutral zone or middle ground (1 Corinthians 6:20).

Possession is one key factor, but there are instances of interference. The best example is if you were a large landowner with title and deed to your property. All because you own the Ponderosa doesn't mean that others won't try squatting on your land. Many settlers in the Old West discovered unauthorized villages established on their ranches. Without searching your soul, you may too have demonic encampments in your life.

Read Psalms 139:23-24 to see where King David went to God searching for sin or anything else that would hinder his pursuit of knowing his Father. It's like a virus scan for our computers. Demonic spirits may not be obvious to you, but God is very aware of them, and will be waiting on you to call out in His name to remove them.

Broken and Blue

Demons are not as powerful as Satan, and simply in no comparison to Jesus. The bible shares stories of possession, but because demons are limited in power and influence, they can only affect certain parts of a person. There is an example of a man living in a cemetery at Gerasenes. They had a pretty good hold over him, but the bible said Jesus cast out a legion of demons. That's six thousand demons, and guess what? They knew who Jesus Christ was and obeyed His every word.

Now just to be clear, not every bad behavior is of the devil or his demons. We can't rely on the old adage that "The devil made me do it," but we have to take this seriously. The devil's the master at deception, so for us to balk at the reality and blow it off as something minor, is exactly the Trojan Horse he's looking for into our lives.

So just how do we find ourselves afflicted with demonic suppression? Demons can't just jump on us. It's not contagious like catching a cold, but there are open access doors that allow for them to squat on God's property until expelled.

1. **Sin** – Left unrepentant, sin becomes a superhighway for demonic access.

2. **Unforgiveness** – We've talked about this before, and that if you don't forgive those who sinned against you, God will not forgive you of your sins. This also brings to mind Matthew 18:34's parable where not only are we not forgiven, but we will be handed over to the tormentors until we repay what is due. The bad news is, we cannot ever repay God for what He has given us. So, unless we want to live a life of demonic tormenting, unforgiving is not an option.

3. **Parental Sins** – These cast generational curses to the third and fourth generation for families that do not accept Jesus Christ as their savior. Legacy sins also open the door to deep past personal pain as well as demonic influence. Forgive your parents, whether they are alive or have passed, and take authority for your spiritual life and legacy.

4. Chemical Addiction – Drug abuse is a complex situation but is one where opening access to demonic influence is common. Addiction is often the result of men struggling to numb their past pain through drugs without focusing on the spiritual healing of their pain. This is also an ample access point for demonic activity.

5. Occult – I think this goes without needing an explanation. Play with fire, and you're going to get burned.

6. Physical and Emotional Trauma – Injury to the body or mind leaves us in a weakened condition. Medications to help the healing process can also introduce us to an altered consciousness. Being aware that you not only have to address the trauma, but the demonic attacks is a great reason to have others stand with you in prayer.

I wanted to cover some of the basic, but most vulnerable, attack points of the enemy. The best way to avoid this is by inviting the Holy Spirit in for a constant inventory check. We focus on situational awareness on the job, yet we stumble through life without taking a close examination of what's going down around us.

Let's also remember that not any one of us has the power or authority over the enemy. Only Jesus holds dominion over Satan and his kingdom. Through the authority Jesus invested in believers, we are commissioned to resist the devil and his demons. The two requirements for us to resist and cast out demonic influence are that we must be a believer and we must use the name of Jesus Christ (Luke 10:17-20). Brothers and sisters, spiritual oppression is real, but God's salvation is eternal.

Call To Action

1. Write out in detail which of the access areas you're most prone to for allowing demons into your life.
2. Write out in detail which types of demonic influence you have experienced.

3. Write out in detail whom you still have left to forgive. This one item will change your life.
4. Write out all personal experiences of demonic interference in your faith walk with Christ.
5. Write out where you see yourself in the supernatural battle within the spiritual realm.
6. Write out a battle plan to prevent Satan from invading your life. Maybe he enters through alcoholism, abuse, porn, or some sin-based addiction or behavior that creates an open door for his indwelling.

13

PERSONAL BAGGAGE

The Spirit of the Sovereign Lord is on me, because the Lord has anointed me to proclaim good news to the poor. He has sent me to bind up the brokenhearted, to proclaim freedom for the captives and release from darkness for the prisoners.
Isaiah 61:1

* * *

I want to share a bit more of my life, and the experiences that brought me to this point of recovery. We've already covered so much, so it's a good time to pump the brakes and reconnect on a more personal level. It's easy to get caught up in the fantasy that the person writing the material must have it all together. Otherwise, how could they write the book, right? Personally, I'm a little wary of a coach who never played the game, a healing mentor who's never been hurt, or a Christian who says they never sinned. I'll assure you I've played the game, been terribly hurt, and I've sinned. Thanks be to God, I'm forgiven, I'm healed, and I'm a victor in Christ.

Broken and Blue

. . .

So, how did I get to the point of writing this book? God called me into service. Well, He didn't exactly tell me to write a book. But He did place a burden for my first responder brothers and sisters on my heart that was so strong, I retired early as a chief of police to pursue His calling. That calling led to ministry and writing this book.

Now to get back on track, when I first met my wife, I carried my suitcase (metaphorically) with pride. It was a high-speed, low-drag carbon-fiber suitcase with shiny wheels that spun like slick glass. I'd adorned the apparatus with big, bold stickers that told the world and her of my worldly accomplishments.

There was no need to reveal the truth to her. Everything I wanted her to know was plastered on the outside of that magnificent suitcase. My favorite stickers read Dad, Police Chief, PhD, Master's Degree, Published Author, College Professor, Triathlete, and Very Single.

They were what defined me and identified who I wanted her and the world to see me as. It was brilliant. I pulled it off without ever having to tug once on that zipper tab. It had to be who I really was if that's how she and others saw me. Right?

We married within the year and looked like we'd perfected the game of husband and wife. It was so simple because she too had a beautiful, shiny suitcase plastered with wonderful stickers.

It took about a year before a strange odor seeped out from my accomplished suitcase. Just to be safe, I kept the zipper tab snugged tight against the edge so nothing got in or out. It was nice and dark inside that case, but it was okay because it had been sealed for decades. And it was magnificent on the outside.

Soon, that odor erupted into a full-blown toxic waste emergency as my once-beautiful suitcase of accomplishments was ripped wide open. Inside the secured darkness was a lifetime of pain, shame, and regret. There was nothing those once-braggart, external stickers could do to hold it together.

I'll never forget the day my wife confronted me. There was a depth of seriousness and sadness I've never witnessed. She asked the question that although I didn't want to hear, I needed her to ask for both of our sakes.

"Are you having an affair?"

"Yes."

That limited exchange released an adult lifetime of hiding a dark secret of my desperate need for physical sex to help me not hate myself. I never understood the overpowering draw for wanting sex, and always dismissed it as just being a single guy doing what single guys do. The problem came when I wasn't single anymore, and I couldn't stop my need for sex.

I agreed to Christian counseling because at the time I wanted to do whatever it took to satisfy my wife. I loved her, but I didn't have the tools to control whatever the compulsion was that drove me away from her in search of others.

I know our first responders' heroic culture scoffs at the thought of going to counseling, but as tough as I thought I was, and mistakenly assuming I was in control of my actions, it wasn't long before my life examined through the reality of God goggles exposed truth for the first time from an objective perspective.

It became clear to me that I wasn't as tough as I was injured. Growing up in a dysfunctional home with a dominant father had left scars on my spirit and a desperation to find love and acceptance where I'd never known it at home. I became sexually active at about twelve years old, and thanks to being almost completely unsupervised, there was no one to mentor me or to tell me that what I was doing was unacceptable.

Women became my drug for easing the emptiness. Only, like any addict, the fix was temporary, and the lows got lower while the risks to keep the highs as high grew greater. Compounding this was the reality of working in a very public profession. I was living a completely bipolar life, and the darkness surrounding the threat of exposure kept me from considering help.

Yet, once again, because of the "golden halo" surrounding first responders, I was able to pursue my need without worrying about possible consequences. I was operating in an environment where promiscuity was the norm. What I suffered as an addiction was revered by my peers as an alpha male. Had they known just how fragile I was, they would've been shocked. Or maybe not.

The effect on my wife was soul deep, and as bad as I wanted to get it fixed up and back on track, healing from this hurt wouldn't be manipulated by my force of personality. It was tough going. There was a lifetime of junk to clean out of that once-glorious suitcase.

I was no longer in command as I'd been almost my entire career. I wasn't the chief, but the cheat. I wasn't revered but was repentant. I was formidable but was begging to be forgiven. It was by the mercy and grace of God that my wife not only forgave me but stood by my side as we attended counseling sessions for almost a year.

When the healing light of Christ was clicked on, every wound suffered and the boatloads of personal pain I'd hidden and suffered from since childhood were gone. I knew my time was running out, and I'm thankful my addiction ended with God's healing grace rather than my suicide.

Transparency and accountability became cornerstones to my healing and recovery from a life of dysfunctional living. The irony of that magnificent suitcase was that it was actually baggage. The stickers were earthly accomplishments I pursued to ease the pain because the sex was no longer enough. I was never going to escape on my own.

It wasn't until I began to heal that I understood that instead of my identity being rooted in what I'd accomplished, it should've been grounded in Christ. Did you notice in the earlier list of external stickers, not one of them read Christian, Believer, Child of God?

That's one of the many things pain does to us. And, because the devil is involved in dividing us from our best relationship with Christ, he makes sure we avoid a foundational identity in Christ.

Truth be told, I knew the junk inside that suitcase. I also knew it stunk because it was my life. But I'd become skilled at keeping it zipped tight and hiding what was ailing me because I'm a cop, and we cannot show weakness, can we?

I believe we're all strolling around with a similarly awesome suitcase decorated with the stickers the stickers that are the only things we want others to see. It's totally understandable that we don't want to air our dirty laundry to the world. But when that world begins to crumble, it's time to consider unzipping it and allowing the truth to come out.

You recall the three things I said I would be wary of? Well, let's add a fourth one. I'd be wary of anyone who claims their suitcase contains no baggage. I mean, seriously, unless you've not started kindergarten yet, you've got baggage. Sometimes sharing yours allows them to unpack theirs. Which, by the way, is why I've written this book.

Let's get started unpacking.

Call To Action

1. Write out in detail what your stickers say about how you identify.
2. Write out in detail what those stickers should actually say to describe you.
3. Write out a laundry list of stinky junk still in your baggage.
4. Write out in detail your commitment to clean that dirty laundry.

14

DISTORTED IMAGE OF GOD

The Spirit of the Lord is on me, because He has anointed me to proclaim good news to the poor. He has sent me to proclaim freedom for the prisoners and recovery of sight for the blind, to set the oppressed free.
Luke 4:18

* * *

If I were a betting man, I'd say this touches home for most of us. Having a distorted image of God has led us away from Him, or at least caused us to keep God at an arm's length. The way we perceive God is tied to a willingness for His hand in our healing. Many of us reject Him because we rely on ourselves. We reject Him because we don't understand Him.

God created family as a reflection of the way His most immediate family shares in a relationship. The Father, Son and Holy Spirit are each separate but the same because of the seamless love shared. Each lifts up and encourages the other in a definite hierarchy of God as the head, Jesus serving His Father, and the Holy Spirit carrying on Jesus's teachings of the Father.

Earthly families were also designed by God for the parents to teach, nurture, and encourage their kids. It is because of the intended intimacy shared between parents and the child, that their first understanding of God the Father is engrained at an early age. This is particularly true of the dad, as he on earth serves as the head of the household and is also called father among his children.

Unfortunately, a negative relationship with our dads has the high potential for causing a distorted and negative perception of God. The reality and most common scenario is that we didn't even understand there was a dysfunctional relationship with our dads. We may never come to know that the way we were treated as kids wasn't what God had intended a parent to show us.

But it's never too late to come into alignment of a right relationship with God the Father. There is a direct parallel between the image of our parents and God. Once we accept that our parents' behavior does not define the nature of God, we've begun to claim a future of freedom from our past.

I'll share from my own experience. It wasn't until many years had passed that I came to understand the dysfunctional environment I was raised in. I grew up in a very blue-collar family with both parents and six siblings. Although my dad was present, he never spoke with me, never said anything nice, and never said he loved me.

I created an excuse that he was the strong, silent type who showed his love instead of speaking it. I guess if dropping me off to ball practice and games was showing love, then yes, he loved me. His silence was in fact dominance. None of us were allowed to express emotion, pain, or fear.

My dad coached high school sports, yet he never once showed me how to throw a ball or swing a bat. He taught for almost forty years, yet never once helped with homework or asked about my grades. This can be the most cruel form of physically present abandonment.

Broken and Blue

As a family, we never once stepped foot in a church. So there was nothing to show me otherwise that God the Father was a present, loving God. While I knew there was a God, my perception of Him was of some big distant guy waiting to whack me when I messed up. Because of that, I found it best to do as I did with my dad by avoiding Him.

When I came to understand that God the Father wasn't like the silent, dominating disciplinarian I grew up with, I had to accept that my dad was to be forgiven, blessed, and honored (Exodus 20:12).

Without an accurate perception of God, we cannot gain true freedom from our past. It's God that sets and keeps us free. If we continue to only see God in the way our parents caused us to view Him, the seamless relationship needed to act as a bridge to freedom isn't possible.

There are seven attributes of the nature of God we must see so there is no doubt that despite our earlier experiences, God is not defined by anyone on this earth. It's an easy trap to remain snared in because dealing with other people is a tangible occurrence as opposed to the spiritual nature of God.

1. God is holy – Holy means that He is separated from sin. Because He is perfect, He cannot look upon us in favor while we carry around unforgiven sin. To draw closer to God, pursue a life of avoiding sin and forgiveness from sin.

2. God is loving and compassionate – The "bigness" of God causes some to see Him as all business without the capacity to love. It is the complete opposite, as God is love, and shows mercy, forgiveness, and compassion like no human ever could.

3. God is unchangeable – While we've experienced changes in our parents with age or circumstance, the one constant in this existence is God. He is the same God who created Adam and Eve, and the same one who waits with loving patience for you to accept Him. He is the Rock.

. . .

4. God is omnipotent – No matter how awesome we might see someone as; they are completely limited in their ability. God, on the other hand, knows no limit. There is nothing He cannot do. God holds authority over the devil, sin, man, and nature. It's sometimes hard for us to comprehend this because His authority is unlimited.

5. God is omnipresent – We men find ourselves in some dark places where the empty loneliness seems unrelenting and hopeless. There is nowhere on this planet or the spiritual realm that God is not present. Brothers, know that in our worst moments, God is there. All you have to do is call out to Him.

6. God is omniscient – Think of the smartest person in history, or the most talented scientist, or even the best game show contestant. The wealth of knowledge, understanding, and creativity is infinitesimal compared to the all-knowing nature of God. He knows the number of hairs on your head and the deepest need of your heart. Just open it up to Him.

7. God is faithful – When God starts a work in you, there is no doubt that it will be seen through until the end. How the end looks is often up to us, but God is faithful. His covenants are eternal and unbreakable. He will never leave you or forsake you, and He is the only completely reliable friend you will ever know.

Whether it was your parents, someone else, or you who created the distorted image of God, it's now your responsibility to draw into an accurate understanding so that you too will know the lasting freedom from your past of personal pain.

Call To Action

1. Write out in detail your first recollection of God.
2. Write out in detail your understanding of God as a child.
3. Write out in detail who most influenced your image of God (good or bad).
4. Write out in detail the nature of your relationship with your parents and how they influenced the way you saw God.

15

DISTORTED SELF-IMAGE

But whoever listens to me will dwell secure and will be at ease, without dread of disaster.
Proverbs 1:33

* * *

Discussing distorted self-images is a super-complex topic. I'm not even going to try pigeonholing each of us into some pseudo-psycho theoretical category. Instead, let's talk about the common issues we face, and how they prevent us from gaining freedom from our past.

   So many people in the public claim cops became cops because they were either bullies in high school or were bullied, so they became cops to have the power to strike back at their tormentors. I might've known a few knuckleheads on the job, but they weeded themselves out pretty quickly. Sure, those were distorted self-images, or possibly lack of confidence in who they were that led to future bad behavior, but I'm talking about digging deeper.

. . .

I was wounded before I ever entered law enforcement. I didn't know that I was until many years later, but I suffered almost daily because of my distorted self-image. Our outward façade projects us as social saviors and moral entrepreneurs, while our personal darkness is shrouded in doubt and pain.

I've known so many first responders in the same condition. Something was fractured in their past, and although the putty they applied when that uniform was worn helped disguise the breaks, it was as obvious in them as it was in me.

Whether it was abandonment, abuse, or addiction, we hold out false hope that time will heal our injuries. Days, weeks, and decades go by and we're still waiting, but now, even worse than before. This tags us with a label of deviance. It's like telling a kid they're dumb. If told enough and without a differing opinion, the kid begins to accept and reflect that label.

Our dilemma is that while society sings our praises, we drag labels of pain, shame, and guilt until the two collide. No matter where the perception of self lands, it's still a misrepresentation of who we are, and who God called us to be.

I'll start off by confessing that this section really hit home. I saw myself in so many of these scenarios. I'd earn a rank promotion or division command and be lauded for that success, while at the same time I was still sitting at home alone hating myself for the guilt of divorces, strained relationships, and a general hatred for the life I'd screwed up trying to live on my own without God.

How many times have you done something wrong, yet tried your best not to do it as you mindlessly walked into the action, and then immediately felt the sick churn of regret as soon as the deed was done? I lived that scenario on a wash, rinse, and repeat cycles for decades. Although I wanted to stop making a mess of my personal life, mostly through bad relationships, I wasn't able to stop on my own.

. . .

Soon, the self-distorted label of failure was attached to my spirit and that's how I saw myself. The night I graduated with my master's degree, there was emptiness, so I decided to pursue a PhD. That was surely going to make me special and feel good, right? Nope. I had barely walked off the stage before my gut was twisting at the darkness of the labels of deviance I'd slapped onto my spirit.

Even the night I was confirmed as chief of police, I looked around the room full of supporters, accepted the shield and commission, and was in tears before I drove back to my house. My refusal to surrender to Christ kept the drain open that swallowed up every hope of being happy. See, there's a difference between being happy and being healed. One ends with the snap of fingers, the other never ends. It wasn't until I shattered my shackles of past pain through Christ that I found healing and joy in the new label covering who I was—child of God.

Let's begin by discussing something I know we all struggle with—*guilt*—which is a response to something we have done. And it's not always a bad thing to experience. Lacking in or having no guilt is akin to sociopathy, and that's a very bad deal.

Guilt is like cholesterol. There's the good kind that produces conviction, and the bad kind that creates condemnation. Our ability to begin the healing process requires that we embrace one as a compass for change, while avoiding the other as a detour to further complications.

Conviction is a healthy response to the guilt we feel when we sin. It's because we are convicted of wrongdoing that we seek a path for redemption and restoration. This path is found through confession, repentance, forgiveness, and renewal. Let me give a simple run down to show the process:

1. Confession – Confessing our sins shows we are aware of the transgressions, accept the consequences of our actions, and take a posture of accountability and transparency so that God is able to work in our lives.

2. Repentance – Is an active term that involves turning away from sin, and having your mind changed about the nature of the activity that involved the sin.

3. Forgiveness – We've talked about this at great length, but if you are the sinner, then we must seek forgiveness from the victim and God. God cannot look upon sin, and without you pursuing forgiveness, He cannot look upon you.

4. Renewal – In Christ we are all new creations. Conviction launches a renewing process, so we continue to grow in our Christian faith. We sin; feel guilty about it; are convicted by the Holy Spirit; so we confess, repent, and pursue forgiveness which all brings us into a position of no longer desiring to commit the same sin-filled act. Thus, we are renewed (evolved) into a believer who is more faithful and draws closer to God's will.

On the other side of the guilt coin is condemnation (Romans 8:1). This leads to nothing helpful for gaining an understanding of what and why we did what we did was wrong, and that through Christ, we are forgiven. All this does is make us feel like failures.

Shame, although closely related, is not the same as above. While the other two results are responses to something done, shame is a response to who we are or perceive ourselves to be. You don't focus on what you've done as wrong, but you center your life on a premise that you are bad. Or in my case, I called myself broken for decades.

The feelings of shame have no cure through conviction, confession, and redemption. It's a label of self-hate that's not easily diminished. You don't just get over being ashamed of who you are.

A friend of mine was called to preach years ago. Yes, he'd lived a pretty rough life, and the reason we'd initially met was because I'd arrested him more than a few times. He confided that he first heard the call but failed to surrender to God's will. Why? Because he was so ashamed of his criminal past.

To be honest, it sort of shocked me. I saw the sweet, genuine spirit nature of the man, but I couldn't get over the criminal man.

Unfortunately, neither could he. He never pursued the call to preach, although he maintained a giving life of a sacrificial servant.

Shame is a powerfully destructive force that cannot be ignored or avoided. It can be your Goliath, which means it can be your God-given victory. It may sound a little cheerleadery, but you must power through the feelings of shame.

Seeing yourself as defective is the height of a distorted self-image. It'll serve as a brick wall in your progress toward freeing yourself from your past. Additionally, shame-bound people may also experience:

1. Denial – Often associated with self-deception, and pain avoidance.

2. Obsessive performance – Used to manage or avoid feelings of shame. Everything in life becomes a test of your worth, and the potential or reality of failure is enough to push you toward suicide rather than face failure.

3. Striving for Perfection – Control and controlling others is common behavior for the goal for perfection. This is an unhealthy pursuit of the impossible, yet the perfectionist subjects others to their harsh expectations.

4. Addictions – Hurting men who avoid or deny they are struggling often turn to ways of numbing the pain. Food, sex, alcohol, drugs are but a few of the "medications" we cling to for relief. Obviously, there is no relief without healing.

I want to also share a condition that we often struggle with as a result of pain and shame. First responders suffer in relationships because they are a tool we use to deal with the hurt. As a result of our dysfunctional childhood or family lives, we desire to be loved and accepted. Except that we don't want to be accepted for who we are, but who we portray ourselves to be, thanks to self-denial and an authoritative uniform that protects that fraud.

But, because we lack the skills to maintain a deep, emotional connection, those relationships end often. Instead of dealing and healing, we move on to the next attempt at love. Of course after a pattern of failures, we feel even more shame, and learn to avoid the deep emotions required for a healthy, adult relationship in anticipation of yet another timely and abrupt end of the relationship. Shame-bound people are desperate for intimacy, but fail to create the environment for attracting, fostering, and keeping it.

The path to healing from the shame that haunts us requires developing four specific behaviors.

1. Recognition – Before we can heal, we must see that there is a problem. Pride and fear interfere with accepting the fact that there is a problem.

2. Determination – Requires repentance and a desire to turn away from sin and destructive practices.

3. Thought-life – One of my favorite sayings is by Albert Einstein, "We can't solve problems by using the same kind of thinking we used when we created them." We must change our way of thinking. You can reprogram your brain through a process called neuroplasticity.

4. Forgiveness – We've talked about this often, and there's a good reason why. God demands it. If not, the consequences are far too dangerous to risk living outside of God's will.

We were created for relationships. Men, especially, reject intimacy although we suffer more without it. While we may decide to wait until we're healed before making connections, the opposite is true in that until we open up and allow ourselves to connect with others in a healthy, adult relationship, we will never know healing and freedom.

I'm not talking about a new girlfriend or wife. These can be relationships restored by God that were once unhealthy connections, or He can provide for new, fresh fellowship into your life. Either way, it's critical that we change the way we see ourselves and our interactions with others. Freedom comes through healing, and healing comes through intimacy.

I knew an officer who had been married eight times. Each ending resulted in that wife just fading away, and the next wife in line would become all the rage. Ever watch an old Tarzan movie as he swings through the jungle on vines? Notice he never let go of one vine until he had securely gripped the next one. That was my friend, and if we think about how we treat relationships, it is us also.

First responders have no shortage of new people coming into our lives because of the nature of our work. But, because we introduce the distorted self-image of who we want them to see, rather than who we are in all of our pain, no relationship, despite its potential, is going to work.

Call To Action

1. Write out ten words that best describe you.
2. Write out why you feel each of these words holds power in your life.
3. Write out Yes or No besides each of the ten words if that's a word your loved ones would use to describe you.
4. Write out in detail what happened in your last romantic relationship, and why do you feel it turned out the way it did–Good or Bad.

16

WRONG RELATIONSHIPS

For you did not receive the spirit of slavery to fall back into fear, but you have received the Spirit of adoption as sons, by whom we cry, "Abba! Father!"
Romans 8:15

* * *

We were made for relationships. I'm going to repeat that—we were made for relationships.

Now, if you're happily married, you'll probably agree. If not, or single, you may wonder what in the world I'm talking about, and why I would emphasize such a statement. I'll show you through God's word why we were created, and that in the creation, relationships were the cornerstone for living a life free from personal pain.

Relationships affect everyone, whether we're surrounded by friends and family or holed up in a maximum-security prison cell. They affect much of the way we are today because of the way we were brought up in the context of relationship.

Before humanity existed, God's relational Trinity (Genesis 1:26) got together and decided to create man in their image. Did you see that? Their image. Talk about a close relationship, God the Father, Son, and Holy Spirit were, and still are, three in one, the Holy Trinity.

This is important because it's the perfect model, and the beginning of understanding why we were created in the first place as expressed in Isaiah 43:7. We were created for relationship. When this is out of alignment with God's plan, it causes dysfunction and personal pain for us.

After God created Adam, they shared a loving, intimate relationship. They hung out together and were maybe the first workout partners who walked together daily. Now, despite being in a position of such honor as God's plus one, Adam wasn't complete. God knew that he wasn't meant to be alone, so He created his helpmate, Eve.

Here is the beginning of human relationship. The connection with God is the first and most important, and with other humans is next. These are the two most important functions for man. Catching a crook in the action or getting promoted to squad captain aren't even close on the scale of what's most important, yet I know we spend more time on those than building the same type of connections as Adam once had with God.

I'll share one more nugget of confirmation about what's our purpose in life, and it's got nothing to do with pay raises, promotions, or pumped-up pecs. Jesus emphasized the relationship need and hierarchy in Matthew 22:37-40:

Let's move on to how relationships affect us in regard to past personal pain and healing. We've already talked about the need to enter healthy intimate relationships in order to achieve real healing. Intimacy doesn't mean romantic or sexual, or even with the opposite sex. Intimate as in the example of God and Adam where nothing stood between them.

. . .

Even if you were a condemned inmate awaiting execution on death row in a maximum-security penal facility, you are still created with the innate desire to connect with man and God. You might deny it, curse it, or avoid it, but it's implanted in you from before your birth. Because it is a soul desire, breaking, disfiguring, or denying it causes pain in life.

To promote this deep desire, God gave us a heart for love, security, and significance. Before sin entered the relationship between God, Adam, and Eve, He was the sole (and soul) source provider for these three needs. It was perfect, and without condition or limitation. The relationship between each was also a sacrificial, giving nature. The spiritual connection with God allowed a free flow of reassurances for these three needs.

Sin broke that communion, and thus man turned away from God and inward to meet his desire for love, security, and significance. It also meant we stopped focusing on the sacrificial model of relationship and began with the selfish, desperate practice of striving to meet our own needs.

How about you take a moment to reflect on each of these and decide for yourself whether each and every single thread of need has been satisfied throughout your life.

It is because of our incessant need to have love, security, and significance that we are never satisfied. A better spouse, more money, and higher promotion are always just beyond our reach. That insatiable itch that you'll never scratch causes chaos in your spirit and an unmet longing in your soul.

Our parents struggled with this, along with every generation back to Adam and Eve. The separation from God because of sin casts a permanent gulf between us. It's within this dark space that our pain was created, and where we'll continue to exist because we cannot provide for our own needs.

Jesus Christ came to redeem what Adam and Eve ruined. In His restoration plan, God also provided Christ as our light that not only saves but heals. Remember, Jesus didn't come to condemn, but to save us. He can provide for our three deepest needs, but we must first ask Him to come into our lives (John 3:16-17).

Instead of spinning our wheels pursuing what we've failed to achieve on our own since the beginning of time, why not put our sights on Christ? He has, does, and always will meet our needs.

Once we experience love that only God provides, we'll understand that love doesn't come through anonymous relationships, security isn't found in a pension or 401k, and significance doesn't come through rank promotions. God's love is supreme, the security of salvation is eternal, and the significance of being His child is the ultimate expression of a space where true healing is discovered.

I believe in working smarter than harder. This is the perfect opportunity to go directly to the source of life and come to know an ultimate love, security, and significance. There's no one on this earth who can provide this to us but Christ.

Call To Action

1. Write out in detail how you would describe your life's experience with love.
2. Write out in detail how you would describe your life's experience with security.
3. Write out in detail how you would describe your life's experience with significance.
4. Write out in detail how different the world would be had Adam and Eve not fallen into temptation and sinned.

17

UNHEALTHY PERSONALITIES

For God gave us a spirit not of fear but of power and love and self-control.
2 Timothy 1:7

* * *

I want to share a bit more about my journey. Our discussion about the need for love, security, and significance really hit home for me. Although I knew what the topic was about and the content, just rereading and writing about it once again brought up old memories. I thought it might help you relate to our focus on the need for relationships, and this part about personality types.

I've shared my story about growing up in a dysfunctional home dominated by an intimidating and distant father. I also confided that we never once went to church, and although I knew there was a God, my only impression of Him was what I saw in my dad. To me, God was a cold, faraway force that was only there to smack me when I messed up.

. . .

Because there was no kindness, intimacy, or love in my understanding of God, I treated Him the way I treated my dad—I avoided them both. It left me right where you'd suspect I'd be, and it wasn't a good place for anyone. It was even worse when I tried to bring a relationship into the picture.

Whether it was a friendship or dating, it wasn't fair to anyone once pain interfered with my desire for relationships. I kept everyone at an arm's length, and when things got strained, and they always got strained, I'd simply pack my pain and move on to the next one. My past was void of openness, kindness, and transparent vulnerability. Those are key elements in any friendship or relationship, and I stunk at each of them.

I was seeking people to fill those voids without the ability to give back to them. I was a consumer of people, but I had no idea how to level the effort with reciprocation. My pain drove the need for temporary fixes to feed the absence of love, security, and significance.

Because I had the spiritual desire for love, security, and significance, I didn't realize I'd desperately set out to find them any way I had to. I dated, and dated, and got married and divorced, and got married on a rebound and divorced, and then over the next twenty years, I dated more, and even got engaged a few times before I ended those catastrophes-in-waiting. I was seeking what only God could give.

I was willing to sacrifice everything to fill those voids that past pain had created. My sense of security wasn't based on God's word, but in money. Supplemental retirements, pension, 401K, CDs: everything available became my obsession so that I'd never have to worry again. Where I lacked family and spiritual security, I decided to replace it with financial security.

The stronghold of money quickly became a daunting weight on my shoulders as I began to sink during an unexpected financial fiasco. I watched everything saved being flushed down the drain. I'd sacrificed a lifetime to secure a financial future because I didn't want to experience the hardships I'd known as one of seven kids being raised on a schoolteacher's salary. Yet, after putting my butt on the line for hours of overtime or off-duty details, everything I'd struggled to save over thirty years was gone.

When we look inward for our deepest, soul-aching needs we will always come up empty. You might be the biggest, baddest guy on shift, or you might even have a family trust fund worth million, but without the light of Jesus Christ, you're never going to know the eternal peace of His security.

It's a miracle how God will move us into one season to prepare us for the next. If you're struggling right now and feel like the pain is too great, too deep, or too dark, please know that God sees you right where you are. Don't turn away from Him in shame. Lift up your face and cry out to Jesus. He will shine upon you and you will finally understand security in this life. Eternal security comes from the word of God, and not some fluctuating stock-market ticker.

The third element affecting our personalities is the need to feel significant. Instead of my significance being that of a child of God, I pursued academics, athletics, and career advancement at a blistering pace. I took pride in the saying, "Hurdle the dead and trample the weak." What a shock it was to realize that I was the one who was weak because I was dead in the sin of my past caused by my pain.

At one point, I'd grown ashamed of every degree, promotion, and accomplishment I'd earned. It wasn't done for God's glory, but that I might feel significant. Ultimately, all I wanted to do was to stop hating myself.

After throwing my earthly crowns to the ground, God showed me that what I gained on earth was to be used to serve His kingdom in heaven. This is what led me to write to you. I know your struggles because I've suffered through them alone and with first responder heroes like you. Who better to share this message with than the men and women I served alongside nearly my entire adult life?

I know we all wish we'd done better or known better years earlier, but the truth is, we can't turn back the hands of time. We can either move toward healing from our past or remain stuck in the pit. A good measure of our forward progress is in our ability to sustain relationships. Because we were created to share a relationship with God and others, we should let that be a marker of true healing.

In addition to being watchful of our own behavior, we must also be aware of others with destructive personality types that might easily derail our progress. Read over these personality types and make a mental note of whether you've run across any or all of them at work. Consider how you get along with them, and whether they add or steal benefit from your life.

These five basic personality types seem to always end up in relational conflict and failure.

1. Peace at Any Price – These people will do anything to avoid conflict, disappointing others, or having to say, "no." They'll also compromise who they are just to gain acceptance from someone else. Usually raised by aggressive parents who employed guilt, rejection, and condemnation to gain compliance, this personality type is mistaken for agreeable and easygoing. There is no consistency with this type because they're constantly shifting to perform. Inconsistency leads to a lack of security for their kids and spouse.

2. Jezebel – Just like the woman in the bible, these people are manipulative and controlling. They do this to have their own needs met and aren't always obvious bullies in accomplishing this. They are very covert operatives in the world of selfish manipulation.

3. Avoider – They are masters at the stiff arm. No one gets in, and everyone remains on a surface level as far as relationships go. Their fear of rejection and betrayal drives this behavior. They've been hurt in the past, and this is their defense mechanism for self-preservation. Meanwhile, they're preserving lots of pain.

4. Cold as Ice – They appear to not need feelings or human contact. How they feel is not a factor in life, but what they achieve is. Workaholics are often found in this personality type. Emotional control usually lies on the surface, as they are prone to outbursts of anger.

5. Performer – They are always on a stage. Most were raised by parents who manipulated love and attention, so they learned to perform for their attention.

These personalities also cross over into multiple types employed by one person at varying degrees. Please, if you see one or a combination of these personality types in yourself, you've got to move toward recovery and restoration. These are destructive types, and not only hurt you but harm so many others.

Breaking free from your past involves recognition. Recognizing your bad personality traits is a huge part of healing. But it's the healing process and the willingness to retool ourselves in God's image so that we are able to pursue sincere relationships that lead to lasting freedom.

Call To Action

1. Write out in detail how your very own testimony relates to our needs for love, security and significance.
2. Write out in detail what you think your personality type is. Do you have characteristics from each or is it only one of these?
3. Write out in detail which personality traits you can and will change.
4. Write out in detail how you feel your childhood influenced your personality.

18

ANGER AND HOSTILITY

In God, whose word I praise, in God I trust; I shall not be afraid. What can flesh do to me?
Psalm 56:4

* * *

When I think about anger and hostility, I recall the countless times on duty when called to someone's house for disturbances. Some scenes were indescribably bloody, while others were a quiet simmer of raging calm. Both worried me, but the quiet ones flat scared me to death because they would snap eventually. And it usually ended up in someone's death.

In reality, anger doesn't always manifest itself in physical violence. We all have anger and experience it differently. Anger is seldom the reason we suffer from past pain, but it's because of the past pain that we are angry.

In today's first responder community, it seems that unless we respond with robotic efficiency, we're immediately recorded and judged as unprofessional or abusive. The stuff we deal with is toxic. We must accept that among the range of essential human emotion is anger.

Anger is an often-misunderstood emotion. Playing the good Christian prevents many first responders from expressing the truth about feeling angry. We're afraid that it's unholy to be mad. I can assure you, and I'll show you in Ephesians, that it's totally cool to lose your cool. Anger is not a sin, unless you sin in your anger.

Jesus was angry when He entered the temple and started flipping tables and chairs. The temple was His Father's house, and it was to remain holy. He even called them a den of thieves (robbers). As we say, and they probably thought so back then, those were fighting words.

But, in His human emotion of anger, it produced a righteousness in a corrupt environment. This would be similar to us getting fired up during a call for service and defending ourselves from a violator who attacks us or our partner. There is justification in righteous anger, and the point I want you to see, is that anger is not a sin (Matthew 21:12-13).

The problem lies more in the way we respond to, manifest, or fail to process anger, than the actual experiencing of the emotion. The apostle Paul gives us the scriptural reference in Ephesians 4:26-27 that it's okay to get angry, but he also gives us the command to not sin, and a timeframe when to resolve our anger, and the consequences for failing to process and release our spirit from the anger.

I'll be the first to admit this is easier said than done. I've lain in bed many nights angry with my wife. My heart is pumping, my body is tight, my mind keeps replaying this verse over and over until all of a sudden it stops, and my friendly neighborhood devil begins reminding me of all the things my wife has done wrong.

Whispers prompt thoughts of how much happier my life was without her. That devil even starts offering names of women better suited for me, and plants bombs of curiosity for finding them over social media. Yep, before I fall asleep hours later, I'm still just as angry, but I have a plan B and C just in case I'm too angry to continue in this marriage. Yet come morning, I can't remember why I'd gotten so mad, but those demonic bombs of impurity are already beginning to explode.

Does this sound familiar? Of course, because it's Satan's number one tactic for ruining our life. Since relationships are so vital to God and our ability to heal, destroying human connections is vital to Satan. I also think this is why Paul was so concise in Ephesians 4:26-27. He makes it crystal clear what is cool, how long God will be cool with it, and what happens if it goes sideways. That's pretty easy to understand. Even for me!

We have to stop shoving everything under the rug. It's creating a boiling point that either erupts little by little or all at once in an extreme violence of uncontainable destruction. Either way, you and those who care most about you wind up in the losing end. Instead try this:

1. Admit that you have anger.
2. Distinguish between healthy anger and destructive anger.
3. Allow yourself to have anger without feeling shame or guilt.
4. Understand what/who it is that causes the anger.
5. Identify whom it is that you're taking your anger out on.
6. Confess your anger to God, and repent.
7. Ask forgiveness.
8. Deconstruct your source of anger to begin the process of uncovering its root cause.
9. Seek freedom from past pains, inner vows, judgments, and soul ties that radiate hate.
10. Speak power over your healing by praying for God's light to eliminate the darkness that breeds anger.

Pastor Jimmy Evans shares eight anchors of anger. They are the most common issues we face when working to overcome anger and hostility. In order for us to overcome the destruction of anger, let's take a look at what causes most of it, and how it binds us to the sin of sinning in our anger.

Anchor 1 – Unforgiveness and Unbroken Judgments:

Seems like the topic of forgiveness pops up everywhere, and for good reason. The more we resent and judge, the angrier and hostile we become. Remember our conversation about passing judgment over others? We often become what we resent through judging. Seek out every opportunity to forgive those who have hurt you, and those who you have unfairly judged. This will take some work, but it's a life-changing chance.

Anchor 2 – Loss and Hurt:

The words from R.E.M.'s song "Everybody Hurts" was on my heart as I thought over this section. Not that I'm a big fan, but the haunting chorus captured the way I'm feeling as I write this. The truth in this life is that we all experience loss and hurt.

Well, everybody hurts sometimes
Everybody cries
And everybody hurts sometimes
And everybody hurts sometimes
So, hold on, hold on
Hold on, hold on
Hold on, hold on
Hold on, hold on
Everybody hurts
You are not alone

Anger at loss and hurt are real. First responders are guilty of trying to shut off the emotional framework and switching gears, but it doesn't work that way. We are human, and we hurt because we also have a spiritual nature. No matter how tough of an exterior we construct, our heart is still connected to Christ.

. . .

We've got to identify situations where we've either experienced loss through death, or through divorce, distance, broken relationships, or any other circumstance that separated us from our cherished ones. The feelings are there, and until we reconcile them with Christ, there is no relief. This is when healing and freedom from past and recurring pain is granted.

Anchor 3 – Fear:

The first time I read this by my pastor, I thought it was crazy. I'm not afraid of anything. Right? I know this might sound nuts, but after I retired from law enforcement, it took just over a year for me to adjust to being a civilian. But, during that year, I developed fears about being alone, being unneeded, unwanted, and basically unable to help others in times of need.

Hold on, because it sounded even crazier the first time I explained it out loud. As a result of those feelings, I developed an unhealthy fear of law enforcement, because not being one of them was what was causing the other feelings of fear. I hated driving for fear of being stopped, ticketed, or arrested. I know it's irrational, but that's what the devil and past pain will do to you.

Of course, my licenses and vehicle were completely in compliance, and I have a habit of being in no rush, so speeding wasn't a possibility, but what was it? It was ultimately a fear of rejection that I had to pray through. Although I honorably retired as a chief of police at the date of my choice, there was still a spirit of perceived rejection from the culture of cops. God helped me to see the cause and the cure.

Anchor 4 – Ignorance:

We almost always develop a harsh reaction to what we don't understand. Sometimes it's a result of feeling intimidated by the person, item, or event, while other times anger may result in disagreement without knowing all of the facts. It doesn't mean we're ignorant, it means we don't understand or have experience with whatever it is that causes us such anger and hostility.

. . .

Racism is a perfect example. Racism is a social construct, not a biological one. In other words, although anatomically similar, the coloring of a layer of skin creates a cultural divide as if we weren't even the same species.

The two sexes are vastly more different than the differences of the skin's pigment, melanin. Yet, we invest the time to learn about women so that our ignorance about gender is erased. If we invested the same effort toward each race, the ignorance would be replaced by education, acceptance, and appreciation. While this wasn't intended to be a discussion of race, it's the most important illustration there is for moving past the anger-producing anchor of ignorance.

Anchor 5 – Spiritual Harassment:
We've already talked about the effect of demonic forces in our lives. Remember, as a Christian you cannot be possessed by the devil, but you can sure be pestered by his legion. Satan hates men because we are God's first human creation, and often our first glimpse of what God the Father is through our dads. Simple—Satan hates you.

Confusion, anger, and hostility keep you from creating and maintaining strong relationships. In that absence of relationship comes the inability to communicate with God or others. This darkness prevents healing from our pain. When you find yourself under demonic harassment, immediately invoke God's authority over the devil and his demons.

Anchor 6 – Unrealistic and Selfish Thinking:
Do we expect more from ourselves and others than is reasonable? What's reasonable, you ask? Do your demands cause stress, risk, or harm to others, or to you? We often push ourselves beyond the safety zone for the sake of an unrealistic expectation.

The result is like overtraining in the gym—negative. Except this isn't a set of bench presses. It's life. When we seek God's will (Psalm 37:4) and His desires for our life, we ensure our own will won't cause or continue past pain.

Anchor 7 – Stress:
Stress is a silent killer. It's lethal and doesn't discriminate.
I feel kinda foolish talking to you about stress. We are experts on what it causes other people to do, how stress makes us feel and what it does to everyone at our agencies. Yet, we do little to address the destructive effects of stress.

Our lives are filled with it, and there seems to be no escape. But, unless we zero in on stress and work to reduce it, the effects of anger and hostility are exponentially increased. This is the space where we're most vulnerable to PTSD, and some of us never recover from the damage.

I used to feed off of stress. At work, the more, the better. In my personal life, my sin created much of it. Because I was surrounded by stress, I thought the ability to handle extreme stress was the measure of a man.

The better measure is to place your priorities straight with a focus on God (1 Peter 5:7), spouse (if married), kids (if you got 'em), and then the necessary things in life like church and work. God's grace provides comfort and peace that the world never can.

Anchor 8 – Lack of Spiritual Enablement:
We, as believers, have been given an incredible gift of the Holy Spirit. It's as if we'd been given laptop computers back in the eighties, or before they existed. Can you imagine the power of the internet back then? I spent so much time digging through my parents' set of Encyclopedia Britannica. I would've loved to have just Googled the information instead.

Jesus told us in John 14:26 that the Holy Spirit would remain with us to remind us of everything Jesus has taught us. The problem is, we fail to plug into the power of the Holy Spirit.

When we walk outside of God's grace, there is a spirit of anger and hostility because we are not practicing the fruits of the Holy Spirit: love, joy, peace, patience, kindness, goodness, faithfulness, gentleness, and self-control. Instead, we're bound by the negative effects of anger over unhealed pain.

These eight anchors can be lifted and released from our lives. But it requires us to face them through prayer, forgiveness, repentance, restoration, and relationships. The first relationship we must pursue is that with God our Father. Trust me, after that, everything else falls into place.

Call To Action

1. Write out in detail describing the last time you went to bed angry. Explain what caused the anger, how you felt while lying in bed, how your feelings or thoughts shifted through the night, and whether your attitude changed once the anger was processed.
2. Write out in detail how you process your anger.
3. Write out a list of the eight anchors. Fill in next to each of those how they affect you, and what you will do to overcome their hold.

19

DEPRESSION

Live as people who are free, not using your freedom as a cover-up for evil, but living as servants of God. ¹⁷ Honor everyone. Love the brotherhood. Fear God. Honor the emperor.
1 Peter 2:16-17

* * *

Depression is another one of those tough topics to cover completely because there are so many facets of dealing with it. There are legitimate medical complications like chemical imbalances that cause depression, and there are demonic harassments, as well as negative thinking.

Over 16.2 million adults in the United States, or 6.7% of the entire adult population, have experienced depressive episodes in the course of a year. Almost half of the people diagnosed with depression are also diagnosed with an anxiety disorder. And it is estimated that a full 15% of all adults will experience depression at some point.

. . .

Although not all suicides are linked to depression, it is a significant partner with very close connections. In the US, suicide is the tenth leading cause of death, and the second among people ages 15-24. This amounts to 44,000 deaths by suicide in 2016. Of those, substance abusers were six times more likely to kill themselves.

In 2016, three times as many officers committed suicide than were fatally shot in the line of duty. Larger metro agencies experience officer loss to suicide at greater rates than normal. In Chicago for example, the officer suicide rate was 60% higher than the national average.

In 2017, 103 active-duty suicides were recorded and since 2008 an average of twelve officers per month take their own life. These numbers only record suicides by active, sworn officers. Reserve officers, retirees, separated officers, animal control, wildlife, prison/corrections, etc. are not recorded as LEO suicides.

The demographic might surprise you, but my guess is that, if you're reading this book, it's something you're very much aware of. In the losses of life in 2017, the average age was forty-two, with sixteen years on the job, and 96% were males.

I'd be willing to bet that we all either know someone who has killed themselves or attempted to do so. It, like depression, is an epidemic in America, and the numbers continue to grow. Are you suffering from a form of depressed feelings because of the pain shackled to your back?

Depression in public safety is derived from two areas – environmental and organizational. First responders receive better training today than ever before. The technology, policy, and opportunities for advancement are tremendous. By the time we're released for duty on our own, we're prepared for the streets.

In studies, the area causing the highest and most unrelenting areas of stress results from organizational factors. Have you ever thought it was more dangerous in the office than on the street? Where levels of destructive stress are concerned, it is. Police and fire services are ranked as being the sixth most dangerous occupations for elevated levels of stress.

I'd like to take a step back from the intensity of discussing the loss of our brethren to their own hands. Let's cover a few major topics, and I'll offer solutions for allowing cracks of light to invade your darkness, until not only is your spirit filled with light, but your pain is healed as well.

Let's start with the most complex because of its medical ramifications—chemical imbalance and biogenic depression. There's no secret that we are an overly medicated society. We can thank big pharma, and doctors who don't understand pain and depression management over the excessive prescription writing that has us over–addicted and under-functioning.

Having worked undercover narcotics for twelve years, I served with the DEA Task Force, and also commanded a regional drug task force during that time. I have a very real insider's perspective of the damage and danger of prescription drug abuse and addiction. Patients claiming depression and chronic pain were the most often cited reasons for doctors to prescribe medication

While there are legitimate causes for medication to manage chemical imbalances, one concern is that the person's significant issues of past pain are not being addressed. When there are issues of abuse, abandonment, self-hate, and the many other problems that arise from a stressed struggle through life, it's vital to combine the medical treatments with counseling (preferably Christian counseling).

Next up is something I think we all relate to, but probably never consider on a personal level. Emotional exhaustion is no different than working hard day after day, and never giving our body the chance to rest. Eventually, the body will begin to suffer from the stress of exhaustion, and performance fades, along with an increased risk of injury.

When I first began my career in the undercover world of drugs and violent crime, I took pride in my ability to endure both physically and mentally. I used to brag that I went ten years without taking a vacation, or sick day off from work. Wow, was I stupid. Sure, I solved lots of investigative cases, but I also suffered two divorces and lost relationships with two sons. The reality was that while almost all of those dangerous criminals are back on the streets, I'm still serving a life sentence of loss.

We need the time off to allow our emotions to relax and restore. One of the Ten Commandments (Exodus 20:8) we all assume is okay to break is the one you'd think we'd clamor to observe.

God is giving us a day off, and we don't even have to burn K-time or vacation hours. But it's not a day to work catching up on stuff, it is a day of rest. The day is for quiet relaxation, meditation, and restoration through worship. This is also the space where angers fade because of the hedge of observing a protective silence on the Sabbath.

While not the same as a chronic, medical condition, emotional exhaustion affects many if not all of us on some level. It might be the death or loss of a loved one, or a major defeat in life such as job loss or failing a promotional exam. Emotional exhaustion doesn't always follow a negative event. Emotional highs such as a wedding, childbirth, or big investigation will have an effect of draining the tanks.

Expect this swing of emotion and combat it with time to recoup. Give yourself a break—literally.

Unhealthy and unbiblical thinking is another cause of depressed feelings. I bet you can name someone who darkens your door by merely standing in it. Sad sacks drain us of life as quick as they drain themselves.

I have a dear friend from a sheriff's office. He's possibly one of my best friends, but every time we talk, he brings up the same old things. It's always negative, and he wants to discuss it to death. It's not that we're looking for solutions to the negative issues, we're just rehashing the unchangeable.

It got to a point where I explained to him that I loved him, but if we were only going to talk about the same negative things, I couldn't hang out with him anymore. Over the following two weeks we sat in silence.

It was a shame, but there was nothing to talk about unless it was that same, negative topic. While I still love him as a brother, we only call once or twice a year. I needed the break from the unhealthy conversations that created a depressed state in my emotions.

Another circumstance common among our fraternity is the feeling that we're losing our mind. I've heard first responders share that they actually thought they were going crazy. They confessed that although they knew better and wanted to do better, they couldn't control themselves from doing wrong. It was usually in the areas of alcohol and sex.

Pornography is the most common trigger when it comes to this lack/loss of control. But you have the psychological and scriptural authority to change the way your mind thinks. Yes, you can reprogram your brain, as we talked about earlier in the book.

The scriptural side of your permission to change your thinking is found in 2 Corinthians 10:4-6. Check out the underlined for emphasis. Paul doesn't say avoid bad thoughts or try smacking them like whack-a-mole. He says take them captive.

As a public safety professional, I know you're aware that the act of taking someone captive is a very active and assertive process. In the same respect, you must assert the authority God has given you to capture unbiblical and unhealthy thoughts and bind them unto obedience in Christ.

Not surprisingly, I found that once we started arresting bad guys at a certain place, they stopped showing up. I also discovered the same to be true when I began arresting the thoughts causing my past personal pain (2 *Corinthians 10:4-6*).

Let's move along to spiritual oppression. We've covered the effects of demonic harassment in detail because it's something we

Broken and Blue

don't usually sit around thinking about, nor is it something we know much about. I feel like we need an anchor to the reality that there is a devil on this earth, and it's not a silly horned goon dressed in red with a pitchfork. You can see it for yourself in 1 Peter 5:8.

And with that sobering fact, we can move forward to better understand the connection between spiritual oppression and depression. In Isaiah 61:1-3, depression is referred to as a heaviness, and as a spirit. The heaviness is also called "darkness." There is no coincidence that Satan's kingdom is described as one of darkness.

Isaiah doesn't just describe the heavy spirit of depression as a darkness, it also gives the cure. The garment of praise is used to describe a constant pursuit of God. Confession plays a major role in praising God. It cleans our heart, spirit, and the supernatural path to an intimate relationship with our Father.

Our last major topic relative to depression, and of course, the pain it carries, is serious discouragement. I'd say that what plenty of people on the fringe of clinically depressed emotions refer to as depression, is actually serious discouragement. It doesn't make it any less severe, but differences in remedies are extreme.

Most of us have experienced this—things just not going right, and there seems like nothing we can do to stop it. That big old diesel engine of discouragement just keeps on chugging down the track. If you've been through a divorce, child custody, unemployment, just to name a few, it becomes very real.

God gives us the example of David, the future king of Israel, in 1 Samuel 30:6-9. Talk about tough times: he was hunted by King Saul, exiled into tough territory, had his wife, kids, and everything he owned stolen, and to top it off, his once-loyal men were now talking about killing him because of the same losses they experienced.

David did what he did best. He wasted no time in turning to God, seeking God's counsel, and acting upon what God instructed him to do. David encouraged himself in the Lord instead of finding a dark cave to play "woe is me." Think about the last time you were seriously discouraged. How'd you bust through it?

We must make up our minds that tough times will come, and situations in life have sucked before and they are going to suck again, but the difference in then and when the decision is yours make today. No matter what may come, commit that you will immediately turn to God, seek His counsel, and do what He tells you to do.

Time to act!!!

Call To Action

1. Write out in detail what you recall about the times you experienced depression.
2. Write out in detail if they were bouts of clinical depression or one of the variations described above.
3. Write out in detail how the bouts ended and whether you took affirmative action or over a period of time solved it.
4. Write out in detail struggles you face where there is a strong mental draw toward destructive behavior (porn, substances, physical abuse).
5. Research neuroplasticity and write out in detail how you understand the process of rewiring your mind as it relates to the list from #4.

20

ADDICTION

For we do not want you to be ignorant, brothers, of the affliction we experienced in Asia. For we were so utterly burdened beyond our strength that we despaired of life itself. [9] Indeed, we felt that we had received the sentence of death. But that was to make us rely not on ourselves but on God who raises the dead. [10] He delivered us from such a deadly peril, and He will deliver us. On Him we have set our hope that He will deliver us again.
2 Corinthians 1:8-10

* * *

Addiction is similar to the term depression. No one wants to deal with it, or even admit that it has a hold in our life. Admitting it, much less talking to others about it, surely has to make us look weak among our lion pride. Right?

Well, I'm not going to tell you what you already know. It makes people uncomfortable when bringing it up. That's why it's such an awesome weapon in Satan's arsenal. I worked undercover narcotics operations for twelve years, and the word addiction was not looked upon with compassion. When it came time for me to face the reality of my own addictions, it was a challenge.

Merriam-Webster defines addiction as the quality or state of being addicted. How much do you love that definition? (Yes, that was sarcasm). Another is the compulsive need for and use of a habit-forming substance (such as heroin, nicotine, or alcohol). Persistent compulsive use of a substance known by the user to be harmful.

I've never met anyone who chose to be an addict. Whether it was drugs, food, sex, alcohol, relationships, or sniffing glue, no one ever wanted their life controlled by a substance or action.

Not only do addicts require ministry, but those who are an important part of their life also require care. We'll talk about codependents later, but for now, please accept that addictive behavior affects everyone within our circle. We might think we've fooled them, but trust me, they are aware, they are suffering, and they are wanting you to get help.

Most addictive behavioral patterns find their roots in dysfunctional family homes. These homes are unhealthy and fail to meet the three most basic needs: love, security, and significance. Since we've discussed them in detail earlier, I'll skim over for the reminder.

We were created with a desire for those needs. God designed our relationship with Him so that He'd meet each of them. He is love, so therefore the relationship is one of ultimate love. Security is found in God's presence, as He is a protective and providing Father. The significance of being a child of God the Father is more significant than we could ever achieve alone.

Adam's break from God's close communion in the Garden of Eden separated us from all three of those needs. Instead of living an outward, sacrificial serving and loving life, we've been forced to find all three of these elsewhere. We usually look in all of the wrong places.

. . .

Dysfunctional homes fail to provide love, security, and significance. Because the desire is spirit led, we cannot choose to not want them met, so we seek to satisfy them by looking outside the home. The absence of these needs also causes pain that continue to burrow and grow until we're forced to medicate it. Satiating pain is what leads us into destructive patterns.

Even if there was zero backstory in our lives and past pain never existed, just the trauma we experience on the job is enough to bring us into an environment of post-traumatic stress (PTSD). Now, take the job's daily grind and the effect it has on the innocent and add it to our burdened past. It's a losing combination, and we can't afford not to break free.

Our methods for deadening pain with unhealthy practices, substances, and behaviors quickly lead to an all-consuming addiction. It's a sly but harsh transition. We don't realize that we're suffering at home until our need for love, security, and significance begins to take hold of our soul. Maybe we act out, or turn inward because the lack of family love, leadership, and acceptance hurts until it harms.

By the time we're old enough to understand that we're not satisfied, happy, or even content, we seek out ways to minimize the pain of not experiencing the love, security, or significance from our family. This is where we enter the addiction funnel. I'll go over each phase that leads to addiction, so you may spot a place where you are, or where you've been. Prayerfully, if you see something familiar, you must stop the train before it barrels forward.

Stage 1 – Experimentation:

Although addiction is complex, the beginning usually starts with curiosity and peer pressure. Whether it's pornography, alcohol, or heroin, no one sees the perceived danger of the behavior at this early point. It might not even be associated with the need to numb your personal pain, but because it alters your state of being, the allure of escape begins.

. . .

Stage 2 – Unconscious Acceptance:

You have accepted that the use of your substance, behavior, or actions is now a normal and beneficial part of your life. You've embraced the stimuli as your own but claim you can walk away at any time. By this stage, you've connected the dots that your pain doesn't affect you while engaged with your acting out. You are empowered by the ability to control your escape mechanism.

Stage 3 – Usage Increase:

This is the point of no turning back. Your obsession has quietly taken control of you, while you indeed thought you were still in control of it. You no longer see it as something you master, but something that masters you. There's no living without it, and you begin adjusting your life to accommodate your addiction.

Stage 4 – Deepest Addiction:

Your life comes second to the obsession. Actually, your life is only lived to feed the obsession. No one matters above the stimuli and you'll stop at nothing to bump up the fading euphoria that is never as wonderful as the first time you engaged in it. You will do anything to get your next fix and will hurt anyone standing in your way.

Let's revisit something about healing. It comes in one of two ways. Yes, God can miraculously heal you in an instant, and the desire, compulsion, or obsession will never tempt you again. Or healing can be a process as in a work in progress.

In the process that is drawn out over time, there are resources available and valuable. Medical treatment facilities are important if required. For example in a case of heroin addiction, before methadone can be prescribed, a medical doctor is required.

During the process of recovering from a physical addiction, support groups and prayers from loved ones are vital for breaking free from the chains of addiction. In the process of healing, there are four areas of required change:

1. Physical Addiction – The source of obsession doesn't matter, although some actions are much more dangerous to your health than others. If your addiction is physical, the goal is to address that before any other issues such as unhealthy relationships, emotions, or thought-life can be repaired. Substance use must be stopped before moving forward in the healing process.

2. **Healing of Emotions** – Repairing emotions is tough. Avoiding pain is what set us on an unhealthy path to begin with. The emotional damage caused because of the past pain must be addressed. Rejection is a main source of the hurt. Working to identify where your pain began is a great place to start with forgiveness so you may experience freedom from the emotion and the pain.

3. **Lifestyle** – Your life reflects your addiction. Your friends, activities, and job, if you manage to hold on to one, all change to ensure your addiction is top priority. In order to heal, everything must change. Yes, especially your circle of influencers. I love this saying, "Show me your friends, and I'll show you your future."

4. **Life Skills** – Addicts become very savvy at adapting so as to feed their next fix. There is a desperation in living life on the jagged edge that makes them take risks and fight to survive for the sake of satisfying their addiction. Once they are free of their addiction, most find themselves unable to function in their ordinary life activities. For however many years you've been living in an addict's fog, that's how many years have gone by without you maturing any further. It makes addicts uneasy and wanting to return to what they see as the simple life.

The key is to identify whether or not we have developed an addiction. Addictions rarely just happen. Alcohol is so common within the fraternity that there's an expectation to consume booze in excess. The average levels of alcohol consumption by male officers (11%) and female officers (16%) are considered "at risk" by the National Institute on Alcohol Abuse and Alcoholism. Another survey of police officers showed 37.6% self-reported one or more problems with their drinking behaviors.

. . .

We're all suffering with not only our past pain, but an inability to end the current hurt. Through Jesus Christ, we can know freedom from painful pasts and all of the ill-gotten behaviors because of it (2 Corinthians 5:17).

Call To Action

1. Write out in detail what addictive or compulsive behaviors you are dealing with.
2. Write out in detail your earliest memories of accessing your addictive substance, product, behavior, etc.
3. Write out in detail what effects addiction has had on your personal and professional life.
4. Write out in detail what steps you have taken to break free from addiction.

21

THE DAILY WALK FORTRESS

Because he holds fast to Me in love, I will deliver him; I will protect him, because he knows My name. ¹⁵ When he calls to Me, I will answer him; I will be with him in trouble; I will rescue him and honor him.
Psalm 91:14-15

* * *

We've carried around backpacks full of past personal pain for so long that we've become hardened against most emotions, hope, and help. Like me: I just assumed I was broken and tried to figure out the best way to get along without hurting too many other people. I wasn't very good at either.

When I broke free from my life of personal pain, it was a flood of emotional reality. I'd discolored my past through a lens of fake memories. I guess all you know is what you know, so when I was able to look back with an objective perspective, the past was actually filled with so much hurt. Forgiveness didn't come easy, but when it did, I was truly free from my past.

. . .

But like any victory in battle, you don't just stick a flag in the ground and celebrate. We must defend our progress and protect ourselves from new attacks. Trust me, if the devil is on your tail, it isn't to wish you well. It shows that you've moved away from his clutches and closer to God. Otherwise, he'd leave you alone as you wallow in his miserable control.

Fortress building is how earthly kingdoms survived conquering new ground and maintaining their presence. It's how you'll defend your newfound territory where the pain of your past remains—in the past.

The first fortress for you to construct is a daily walk with Jesus Christ. If there is to be true freedom from your past, then your personal relationship is the singularly most important aspect of your efforts. Without Christ, there is no lasting freedom from pain, nor is there genuine healing.

God's salvation is a gift (Ephesians 2:8-9). There's nothing in this life that can earn it or deserve it. Trying to do so is an insult to the gift-giver: God. How we protect that gift also says volumes about how we feel for the gift-giver. So these fortresses not only protect our freedom, but they show God the Father that we do love Him for the gift of salvation through His son Jesus Christ.

Any good relationship requires work. It's not uncommon for us to come into a relationship with Christ as our Lord and Savior, only to have the initial excitement and fire for Him to fade until we're back at a point before we knew Him. Why? Unless we're mentored on the three most basic ways of pursuing that relationship, it'll diminish in intensity.

Praying, Reading, and Submitting are the keys to a vibrant Christ-led life of freedom.

It's easy to get overwhelmed and intimidated by the inconceivable sovereignty of God. It blows my mind that He created it all, yet He still wants to know me. I mean really, who am I that He would want to pursue a relationship? I always think back to King David, who asked the very same questions.

Then King David went in and sat before the Lord, and he said: "Who am I, Sovereign Lord, and what is my family, that you have brought me this far?
2 Samuel 7:18

The truth is relationship is the very reason God created us. So, yes, God does want to be our best bud, and if we'd stop running, ducking and trying to jive Him, we'd enjoy a relationship that holds more promise and blessings than ever imaginable. That closeness comes through communications—prayer.

God not only wants us to pray, but He promises to hear and answer our prayers if we come by faith. I've had first responder friends ask why God didn't just heal them when they prayed for it.

God does hear our prayers, and like we've talked about before, there are two ways of healing: instant miracle and by process. For those of us who went through an entire process, it doesn't mean God gave more weight to other's prayers, or that yours weren't strong enough.

It meant for me that there was so much past to get past, that I would've missed processing and sorting out relationships, feelings, and a clear perspective going forward. God guards our hearts, and I know without a doubt that had everything been dumped on me at once, I would've been devastated instead of liberated.

The next step to reinforcing an invincible fortress is to read God's word every day. The bible is unlike any book. You don't read the Bible; the Bible reads you. It makes God's word come alive, and plants His intimate desires for your life deep into your heart.

What you water your soul with will bear the fruit of that word. Years ago, I used to read news the instant I woke up. Of course, everything is so biased and negative that even before I'd stepped foot out of bed, my attitude would reflect a hardened, pessimistic tone. Reading God's word in the morning's quiet time sets my head and heart apart if for only a moment in time, but it positions my attitude for the remainder of the day.

. . .

The third, and final part of structuring your fortress is yielding to the Holy Spirit. Unfortunately, the Holy Spirit is like the George Harrison of the Beatles. Unknown and often forgotten for the sake of God the Father and Jesus Christ, the Holy Spirit is the third and equally important part of the Holy Trinity.

The Holy Spirit's role is usually misunderstood, and therefore not given the attention of pursuing a relationship with Him. In John 16:7-15, Jesus tells His disciples that He must go so that the Comforter may come. He explains who and what the Holy Spirit is, and why it's necessary. Today, the Holy Spirit's role is just as vital and alive as when He fell upon the people at Pentecost.

If you haven't up to this point in life, please begin to pursue a relationship with the Holy Spirit. You aren't cutting God out of your worship by doing so, you are plugging directly into His power. The Holy Spirit gives us God's power (Acts 1:8) and fills us with the character of Christ (Galatians 5:22), so we may have gifts for ministry (1 Corinthians 12), to comfort us (John 16:7.)

I want to share 1 Corinthians 12 with you because it's the complete explanation of who the Holy Spirit is. This is so important to understand because I've known people who thought the Holy Spirit was an angel or a myth. Trust me, but more important, accept God's word, that the power of God resides in the presence of the Holy Spirit. I've underlined the gifts of the Holy Spirit for reference in *1 Corinthians 12*:1-13.

My friends, these are the three most important things you can do to ensure that you break free from your past, and that you stay free.

- Praying
- Reading
- Submitting

These building blocks will make your fortress invincible against the attacks of the enemy. Please commit the time to pray, read, and submit daily. You will come to know the Holy Spirit as your best ally and friend.

Call To Action

1. Write out in detail what you understand praying to be. Think through this and try to deconstruct how you think about prayer in your life.
2. Write out in detail what you like and don't like about reading the bible. What draws you to it or keeps you away from it.
3. Write out in detail what role you understand the Holy Spirit to play in the Holy Trinity.
4. Write out in detail how and when you will make the time to pray, read, and submit on a daily basis.

22

THE TRANSFORMED MIND

He has now reconciled in His body of flesh by His death, in order to present you holy and blameless and above reproach before Him.
Colossians 1:22

* * *

I've been fortunate to have traveled a bit outside of the United States, and to experience, among other things, the ancient ruins and early century forts, castles and blockades built as defensive weapons against attacks of war. Some of the most incredible structures imaginable were never once tested in combat, and still sit peacefully at attention over a time gone by.

Why weren't they used? Because their very presence served as a greater deterrent than any number of warriors or weapons piled behind it. They were steady in getting ready and the enemy knew they weren't up against some village of rock throwers. It's no wonder most of these kingdoms and countries survive still today.

. . .

When we talk about readying our fortress with praying, reading the bible, and submitting to the Holy Spirit, we are building a defensive posture in our daily walk with Christ. The further we pull away from the bowels of Satan's suppression of past personal pain, the more involved he and his demons become in getting you back into a crooked environment.

Also, not to say that every bad day, flat tire, or headache is of the devil, but strengthening your tower will also help defend you from getting distracted by life's everyday drama. Now, I can't promise you won't get upset if your favorite team loses, but your fortress is your protection.

I've purposefully mentioned defensive protection because I want to now talk about offensive weapons. The most important weapon we have in the fight for freedom is our mind. It is an incredible machine and a super-computer that by all scientific estimates is only performing at 10% of its intended capacity. As magnificent as the human brain is, it serves as a blessing and a curse to most of us.

Our ability to transform our mind is the next important piece of the fortress-building process. The fuel for the shift from a carnal-driven organism into a spiritual weapon is God's word. There are a few sayings that apply here: "Garbage in, garbage out" is one of them that holds true.

Feeding our brain with the liberal media's diet of movies, television, news, and social media causes the brain to operate in a chaotic stream of sex, violence, and an abnormal appreciation of the world we live in and others imagined. Cursing and talking about the vile things of this world burns brain potential, as does gossip and speaking wicked of others (*1 John 2:15*).

This is the brain's own process of rewiring or reprogramming itself. It's the real deal, so check it out if you want more information. But the reality of it is, you have the power to retrain your brain. Let's back up to the saying above about firing and wiring. Heroes struggling with pornography tell me they have tried to stop their consumption, but their cravings are too strong. They're trapped in a rut, with no hope of freedom from an addiction caused by early pain.

A porn addict's brain actually experiences change because of chemical activity released while craving, and then watching pornography. Because of the chemical reactions, your brain rewires itself to focus on satisfying its need for graphic, sexually visual stimulation. Soon, it only desires the fantasy stimulation, and real, physical sex has little to no appeal.

I've been told that they were addicted to porn because that's the way God made them. Can I tell you that's a load of junk? You were not born with an innate need for porn. Porn didn't become an issue until exposure, and with that exposure soon comes the addiction. Why? Because that was what you fed your brain, so it programmed itself with the fuel it was being fed.

The diet of pornography exposure doesn't come as a result of sexual prowess, it is a result of a deficit in your spirit. Rejection, abandonment, and abuse are but a few reasons that send good-intended kids and adults searching for a fix from pain's reality.

The great news is the brain can be rewired. It depends on what fuel you use to supercharge it. Prayer to get your brain into a supernatural nature is the primer, and daily bible readings are the high-octane fuel that gets your thought-life steered in the right direction by the Holy Spirit.

Transforming our mind serves the purpose for connecting us to Christ today and in the future as we grow closer in our walk with Him. Our thoughts are a gateway that tethers us to our past, and tap into the painful memories we recall, or unconsciously suppress.

We cannot truly be free and connected to Christ if we continue fueling our thought-life with things of this world. Satan will continue to flood our minds with distractions about failures, doubts, past sins although God has long forgiven and forgotten them, and new temptations to lure our thoughts away from the word and the works of God.

Let's consider the devil's favorite attack tactic: messing with our mind. He got into Eve's head smack dab in the middle of paradise. In Luke 4:1-13, he also tempted Jesus in the wilderness for forty days. Satan couldn't and wouldn't lay a finger on Him, but he gave it his all to tempt Jesus into thinking about sinning. Of course, Christ was never tempted or considered falling for the lies, but what's important for us to know is it was also a mind game.

The devil promises stuff he doesn't own and can't deliver. Why do we call him the father of lies, yet accept what he says as the gospel truth? When he plants doubt over our recovery and freedom from the past, we succumb to his lies. When we commit to seeking help for what hurts us, he tells us that it's a secret, so we keep our mouths shut and suffer in silence.

There's no need to sit on the sidelines where your thought-life is concerned. Paul makes it very clear that we are to take an active, possessive posture over anything entering our minds. Don't just allow it to noodle around in there or wait for it to take hold before trying to redirect your thoughts. Snatch the illegitimate thought up and own it by bringing it into submission to Christ (2 *Corinthians 10:5*).

There are so many benefits to transforming your mind into a spiritual fortress for your war against a painful past. Consider what we've discussed, and I pray you will gain an appreciation for the role of your mind in the war for independence from past pain.

Think about it!

Call To Action

1. Write out in detail what thoughts slip into your mind the most that you'd have trouble explaining to your wife, loved ones, and Jesus.
2. Write out in detail how you handle those thoughts.

3. Write out in detail what fuel you use to feed your thought life.
4. Write out in detail what information you can meditate on to recharge spiritual thinking.

23

ACCOUNTABILITY

"Out of my distress I called on the Lord; the Lord answered me and set me free."
Psalm 118:5

* * *

I was sitting in the back seat of a friend's pickup truck as we returned to the church's parking lot after lunch. Another friend in the passenger seat hopped out so we could pull in closer to a barrier, which gave us room to get out on the driver's side. It was just two of us left in the car. My friend looked back at me through his rearview mirror and asked, "Do you mentor men?"

"No," I blurted out, completely caught off guard.

We both climbed out of his truck in silence. I regretted my response, but at the time I had not ever mentored anyone. To myself, I thought, who am I to hold anyone else accountable? I'd had my own problems and felt lucky enough to escape without having them destroy me.

. . .

Soon I learned that it wasn't my job to hold others accountable, as much as it is for me to help men hold themselves accountable. Too much of the other way, and it devolves into judgment of someone else's behavior. Being an accountability partner wasn't what had scared me, it was not understanding the difference in the relationship between two brothers. Accountability is an honest reckoning of self-judgment, while a partner is there to monitor with an objective perspective, and gentle, encouraging words.

So, what is accountability? A few men I know through the ministry used to describe it as ratting yourself out to God. I used to laugh and tell them that would be confession, but they were close. Although I knew the term ratting out was more of a joke amongst them, the intention of making known what was done, was absolutely on point (Romans 14:12).

In the context of breaking free from our past of personal pain, the term accountability conjures up what my friends used to joke about. The negative connotation associated comes from disciplinary uses. Back in grade school, on the job, civil and criminal codes, and in church, all we've ever known is the reactive nature of being held accountable.

No wonder no one wants to hold themselves accountable. I guess my friends were right on another level. When applied in a negative "gotcha," after the fact, it loses its appeal and application for the sake of what we're working to accomplish.

Let's look at accountability another way.

What if we instead looked at accountability in a positive light? If instead of it being a tool to retro-discover failures, we front-load success by clearly identifying the expectations ahead of time, and then apply accountability measures as a means to progressively monitor and mentor the entirety of the journey.

I was not, and never will be, a good runner. Especially not a fast runner. Even while training for triathlons and half marathons, my running philosophy was start slow, end slower. But in run training, the timed splits are vital. They are a front-end goal loaded for potential success.

Let's say you are running the mile on a standard high school track. That will be four laps until you collapse into a heap of air-sucking gratitude that it's done. But if you want to set a new record, then you know that there is a goal pace for running each of the four laps.

Running slow around lap two doesn't mean failure, it just means you have two more laps to pick up the pace so that by the checkered flag, you'll have brought yourself back into alignment aimed at victory. Do they actually wave a checkered flag in running?

I'm not sure because I've never come close to finishing first, but I hope you get the idea. Accountability is important, and scripturally necessary for keeping ourselves on the path toward obtaining whatever goal we've set before us.

We also achieve our goals more often when we work with an accountability partner. Not a taskmaster, or judge, or disciplinarian, but in the biblical description from Galatians 6:1-5 of a brother or sister who cares about you and is as invested in your success as you are.

I know you might prefer holding yourself accountable as opposed to opening up to others. It's embarrassing to ask for help with a personal problem. It can be downright mortifying to share the details, but God encourages us in James 5:16 to not only hold each other accountable, but to also confess our sins to one another for healing.

Don't allow the shame whispered into your ear by Satan to continue your failed attempts to break free from secret pain. Hiding your sin, addiction, and hurt from others is exactly what the enemy wants you to do. Suffering in silence is not living. Although not scripture, I use this quote often as it once helped me to realize that I didn't have the resources to do it myself.

"We can't solve problems by using the same kind of thinking we used when we created them."
~ Albert Einstein

We need each other. One on one, prayer groups, small groups, online, or the many other opportunities to submit your goals of breaking free from past pains before other believers are great options. It's a valuable way of increasing your ability to stop the destructive behaviors that have shackled you to the past, while encouraging the positive changes that ensure freedom.

Heroes, get connected.

Call To Action

1. Write out in detail what your experiences with accountability have been: good or bad.
2. Write out in detail what goals you would share with an accountability partner.
3. Write out in detail what goals you would not share with an accountability partner.
4. Write out in detail a list of men, and their contact information, that you would feel close enough to for serving as an accountability partner.

24

BOUNDARIES

Grace and peace be multiplied to you in the knowledge of God and of Jesus our Lord; [3] seeing that His divine power has granted to us everything pertaining to life and godliness, through the true knowledge of Him who called us by His own glory and excellence. [4] For by these He has granted to us His precious and magnificent promises, so that by them you may become partakers of the divine nature, having escaped the corruption that is in the world by lust.
2 Peter 1:2-4

* * *

"It was just one peek," said one of the men I worked with in law enforcement.

"And what happened?" I asked.

"I relapsed," Todd sighed.

There was no judgment or condemnation of this man. Todd had struggled with pornography since he was twelve. After repeated sexual assaults by his stepfather, he was rejected by his mother when he sought her rescue.

Abandoned emotionally, Todd was left empty, aching, and alone. After Todd and his mother were dumped by the sex offender, the only ones who made him feel loved and safe were the actors in his pornography.

Todd had worked with counselors for years to overcome his addiction. He'd broken free for about two years and managed to forgive his mother and stepfather for the horror inflicted on a once-young and promising future. Todd connected with me about six months before his relapse because he'd begun to feel alone following his second divorce and sought an accountability partner to help him stay on the rails.

He also suspected that his police department was closing in on his addictions and sought reassurance that he was making the right moves to avoid further temptations that always led him back to pornography.

One of the first things I helped Todd establish was boundaries. He was already familiar with the concept. With Todd, it wasn't as much of a challenge to get him to identify his challenges, as it was to encourage him not to cross over them.

Todd was like so many of us in public service. His work, reputation and acceptance among peers was so important, that he couldn't accept the reality of being exposed for his weakness or inability to remain within his boundaries. That was the last conversation Todd and I would have. I couldn't bring myself to attend his funeral.

Boundary setting for first responders can be seen as an insult and restriction to the alpha personalities that send us running toward danger while everyone else flees to safety. We are conquerors after all. Like a yard dog with an electronic fence, we don't like being boxed in. Of course, this is also what gets us into most of our troubles.

My wife had a great way of explaining that you create boundaries to protect what you love, while keeping the threats on

Broken and Blue

the outside. She is correct. Boundaries are meant for our protection. Cells are created for our confinement.

There was only one boundary at the very beginning of creation. According to Genesis 1:28, Adam and Eve were free to roam the entirety of paradise. Talk about a sweet deal: they were placed in charge of everything God had personally created.

Except for the one and only boundary, Adam and Eve had nothing to worry about. God made it easy and told Adam to eat from any tree in the garden except the tree of the knowledge of good and evil. With that one boundary set (Genesis 2:15-17) for everyone's own good, God left them to enjoy the literal fruits of His labor.

You see, just like Todd, their attention didn't seek the freedom of choice and the unlimited number of other alternatives. No, Satan wants you to cross that line. He can't shove you across it, but he sure will get inside your head to consume your thoughts with nothing else but what's been set outside of your boundary.

Todd was no different than Adam, and they're no different than any of us. We want what we can't have. But there are reasons why we can't have certain "fruits," and of course there are consequences when we take that bite out of those that are forbidden.

Following up on the example of Adam and Eve, not only did they violate the boundary and lose their intimate connection with God, but there was another boundary established that they were forbidden to cross. Of course, it was the entrance to the Garden of Eden, and this time God ensured it remained beyond their reach with the help of an angel and flaming sword. Yes, some decisions come with greater consequences than others (Genesis 3:24).

How fired up do you think Satan was once he saw Adam and Eve on the outside of paradise and God's will? Yep, the same amount of happiness that he felt when Todd logged into that porn site. What do you do that brings a smirk to Satan's face?

. . .

We've got to either set boundaries for ourselves, have help in setting them, or have someone set them for us. There are different scenarios, but all include respecting the purpose of boundaries, and the potential consequences for breaching them.

When we look at the big picture, I'm not sure why we are so averse to the idea of boundaries. They are everywhere from speed limits on the highway to the number of calories on a diet. Boundaries shouldn't be seen as limits to our fun, but standard bearers for achieving success, or simply having a good, safe time.

Where are you in need of boundaries?

- Pornography
- Alcohol
- Drugs
- Foods
- Sex
- Texting or social media
- Locations such as strip clubs or bars

I was talking with a counselor one day and he shared a story about a client who had overcome his bondage to sexual sin. The man had spent his life savings at strip clubs and on prostitutes. The counselor said the man was so excited that he'd been free for a while and wanted to pay it forward. The man's idea was to preach the gospel to the strippers and hookers at the clubs in his area.

The counselor laughed and said that was a resounding no. He had to explain to the man that he'd forfeited the ability to witness to women in those environments, because they were beyond his boundary. In the world of recovery and freedom, you really can't have your cake and eat it too.

I suggest you get help in establishing boundaries to ensure you break free and stay free from the pain of your past. It's easy to focus on avoiding the obvious, but there are many other areas you may not realize that remain threats to your freedom.

Without an objective perspective, you may not see the people closest to you that serve as triggers for breaking boundaries, locations that remind you of the "good old days," or activities that are just waiting to reel you back in. Although we've already talked about the difficulty in confiding in others, it's going to be necessary for identifying a set of boundaries that are for your good and your success.

Here's to protecting the good stuff.

Call To Action

1. Write out in detail all boundaries you already have in place.
2. Write out in detail whether you've honored or broken each boundary, and if broken, include a detailed explanation why.
3. Write out in detail what boundaries you need to set in place, and why.
4. Write out the names and contact information of the people in your life who would be best for helping you establish boundaries.

25

CONSEQUENCES

For God so loved the world, that He gave His only Son, that whoever believes in Him should not perish but have eternal life. [17] For God did not send His Son into the world to condemn the world, but in order that the world might be saved through Him.
John 3:16-17

* * *

I always told my kids, "Decisions and Consequences."

As they grew older, they'd laugh and say, "We know, decisions and consequences." Those two words brought almost as much joy as my three favorite words, "I love you."

Decisions and consequences go together, and if there was any other measure by which to use when deciding between one thing or the other, it's invaluable. For me, personally, it was also confirmation that what I probably repeated a thousand times had actually stuck in their heads.

We've purposefully covered what I like to call the Spiritual A,B,Cs over the last three sections. Accountability and Boundaries were explained and encouraged for use in a positive way for promoting your success in freedom from your past. I'm going to flip the concept of consequences upside down, but only about halfway around. Consequences without teeth really offer little support toward your goal of healing and freedom.

Also, the truth is, consequences are usually out of your control. Criminal actions result in consequences handed out by a judge, work violations are handled by a supervisor, and family indiscretions are addressed by your wife or other members.

I can't in good conscience water down the importance of consequences. We face them every day: from waking up late and missing work, to failing to identify our pain and continue living in misery. The only upside is that we really hate receiving discipline, so we try harder to remain on the rails to avoid the punishment of consequences (Hebrews 12:11).

If you're like me, we reach a point in our misery where the consequences no longer matter. The pain is so great and the need to numb it is so intense that you almost find yourself wanting to get busted in hopes it goes away. We get to a level where we've been hurting for so long that no consequence short of death could make us feel any worse about ourselves.

That's a very dangerous point to fall into. I know; I was there. The problem we face is that we've fought to survive the pain, so there's been a resilience developed over the years. Our weakness has been calloused over for so long that besides being numb, we also become very hardened. The most hurtful thing becomes the reality that we're trapped in that lifestyle, and no matter how bad we want to do better, to feel better, to be better—we can't.

After the defeat of our spirit and the surrender to living a life controlled by our past pain and current efforts to avoid it, how do we use consequences to our benefit? There are certain influencers that motivate us in everything we do. We're here and committed to this book because we need answers, explanations, and motivations to finally break free and stay free.

. . .

There are two ways to best use the concept of consequences, since the reality of it has little bearing in our life, or even death. Consider what our actions do to others. Start with a series of concentric circles. Maybe the outside circle includes your work acquaintances. The next ring holds your friends, while the one inside of that includes extended family. Next would maybe be your kids, and the one after that is your wife. Of course, the smallest and most affected circle is you.

While you can cross out the innermost circle representing yourself because consequences don't move you to change, how about looking at all of the other people in our life who get screwed over because we can't pull it together. I'd suggest you actually draw out this visual. It's stunning when you see that there's more than just you invested in your healing.

The other option for helping the concept of consequences to maintain a sense of value in your life is to understand that the entirety of your life is the consequence of other people failing you. This may be the only way for you to comprehend the bigness of just how important consequences are. I'm not trying to lay a guilt trip on you, but I don't want to give up on helping you to pierce your heart for the reality of cause and effect.

Because your life represents the consequences of someone failing or harming you, the life of pain and dysfunction has become your normal. If you bring anything away from this message, please let it be this: you are not responsible for what hurt you in the past, but you are responsible for how you respond to it today.

Suffering like we do is not normal, nor is it scriptural. You do not have to accept the life you live as all you can experience. God created us for so much more. Don't allow the consequences of pain, shame, and guilt take God's glory away from you.

Call To Action

1. Write out in detail what you understand the consequences of failing to heal from your past pain will do to your life.
2. Write out in detail the last consequence you paid as a result of trying to deal with your past pain.
3. Create the drawing described in the content and include as many circles with names affixed as your life connects to.

26

RESTORATION

But the one who looks into the perfect law, the law of liberty, and perseveres, being no hearer who forgets but a doer who acts, he will be blessed in his doing.
James 1:25

* * *

We've come a long way together. If you've powered through each of these last twenty-five chapters without stopping, great going! If you had one or a few stops along the way thanks to that old thing we call life, or getting slammed with callouts or report writing, still, great going!

The point is, all that matters is you are here. Breaking free from our past is a process. It involves so many things, but healing freedom is our goal. You are now aware that when we discuss healing that God either heals through miracle or a process of faith-building patience and persistence.

Healing is often used by God to draw out flaws or strengthen certain characteristics in the sufferer and their close allies. It's not nearly as immediate as a miracle, but the end result is just as solid. We become so naturally bonded to our partners and other first responders that we may not even notice how they are blessed as we move toward freedom.

Healing is also about restoration. There are various types of restoration, and the act of restoring us is a vibrant dynamic. One definition of the word restoration is "the action of returning something to a former owner, place, or condition." Another is "the process of repairing or renovating a building, work of art, vehicle, etc., so as to restore it to its original condition."

Do either of those apply to you? In our restoration, we are being returned to our original owner—God. A crafty car thief can steal your ride, change the VIN numbers, and apply for a new title, but that still doesn't make it his car. Maybe we took possession of our own lives and walked away with the deed and title, but self-ownership wasn't what was intended when the creator crafted us for this life.

The other definition describes being repaired and renovated, so as to restore to its original condition. I love how this secular definition fits so perfectly into God's design. Our original condition was Adam.

Honestly, we've moved the needle a long way from those earliest days, walking nude with lions in the Garden of Eden. But thanks be to Christ's sacrifice for our salvation, He is the second Adam, and thus a hope restored for living a Christ-like life.

I talk with first responders all the time who feel as though they lose a layer of who they are each time they sin and ask for forgiveness. It takes them a while, if ever, to understand that when God forgives them, they are fully restored. As in the old hymn says, *"What Can Wash Away My Sin?"* We aren't almost white as snow, or beige or even eggshell, we are washed white as snow.

What can wash away my sin?
Nothing but the blood of Jesus;
What can make me whole again?
Nothing but the blood of Jesus.
Oh! precious is the flow
That makes me white as snow;
No other fount I know,
Nothing but the blood of Jesus.

Let's also be very blunt at this point. There are some who assume because they are forgiven of sin, that it's a blank check to live as they wish, and sin again because they know God will forgive them again and again and again.

Being forgiven by God requires more than a plea in a time of panic. God demands confession, repentance, and a contrite heart toward change. If you ask forgiveness because you feel sad over what you did or got caught doing, and not because of the hurt you caused others and pain brought to God, then you are still beyond the spiritual realm of God's loving nature. Having a teachable spirit got you through the basic training academy, and it will get you into God's will and grace.

Restoration is such a vital word in this conversation, because it's exactly the process of not only being washed white as snow of your transgressions, but returning to the original owner and creator, God. That is forgiveness and restoration.

Brothers, restoration is where we want to be, and where we want to stay. God will not take you back in time to a place before you were hurt, but He can restore you to a posture of a pain-free life. We must initiate the pursuit of restoration with the elimination of unconfessed sin.

Adam was in paradise in God's presence in what we know was the Garden of Eden. He was provided everything including the intimacy of Eve. Sin for them, just like for us, separated us all from God's presence.

How drastically different do you think Adam's life was without God's constant presence and relationship? How different are our lives while in the midst of the sin we commit thanks often to carrying around our past pain? Through restoration we have been given the gift to draw near our Father once again. Yes, we've experienced pain in our life even while we walked by His side, but He is there to move us through the process.

God knows our hearts but won't force Himself into them without our invitation. We have free will, and because of that free will, we must choose to accept God's love. That even goes for the most ardent believer. He is actively waiting to come into your life, but we must be open to restoration.

This is a tough process, and chances are, you're doing this alone or have maybe confided to your spouse or someone very close to you. There have been days I know you might've just closed the cover and moved on, but there was also something that said, "Don't quit."

That's the voice of God, and you are hearing it because He loves you and doesn't want to lose you any longer than He already has.

Our pain, while it mostly came as a result of someone else's sin, has caused us to branch off into sinful behavior while fighting to combat the pain from our past. This is our time to close the gap and restore life as God intended it to be lived (Acts 3:19-20).

Call To Action

1. Write out in detail about something that you have restored. Maybe it was a car, furniture, a picture, a hobby, or a relationship. How did it make you feel?
2. Write out in detail what it is that is broken in your life, and in need of God to restore back to its glory.
3. Write out in detail sinful behaviors that you still

struggle with, and your plan to commit them to God for repair and restoration.
4. Write out in detail what you envision a restored you to look like.

27

RENEWAL AND THE FORTRESS AGAINST SPIRITUAL WARFARE

Since therefore the children share in flesh and blood, He Himself likewise partook of the same things, that through death He might destroy the one who has the power of death, that is, the devil, [15] and deliver all those who through fear of death were subject to lifelong slavery.
Hebrews 2:14-15

* * *

I love the bible's imagery of war, battle, and armoring up for the fight. God calls it like it is—it's a war—and as the saying goes, war is hell. Well, in this case, we are at war with hell's legion of demons. But, unlike earthly encounters where victory is never certain until the battle is done, we already know who raised the flag of victory.

Jesus Christ reigns supreme because He's already won the war. And by His authority over Satan, we are victors too. Then why are we still struggling, you might ask, and why does it sometimes feel like we're losing? It's simple, the devil doesn't throw victory parties for believers. He's also tenacious and refuses to give up until he's finally locked away in the lake of fire (Revelation 20:10).

So, until then, we have to care for the fortresses we've constructed for God's kingdom and our freedom. The fortress of spiritual warfare is something many believers figure they'll just avoid for the time being. The reality of a spirit realm still seems a little too made-for-movies. But the reality is, we live in both a natural and supernatural realm. Our daily existence is in the natural, and this is where every ounce of our past pain originated. When we pray and communicate with the Holy Spirit, we enter the spiritual realm.

God gives us everything we need for spiritual warfare. It's His suit of armor, and it is invincible. Not even RoboCop or Iron Man can hold a candle to God's armor. Our battle to gain independence from our past isn't against other people. No one can make you live in your memories. Sure, they can remind you of certain times in your life, but they don't hold the power to return you. These shackles remain entrenched in your mind and is why transforming your thought-life is critical to freedom.

If you are battling people over your access to your past pain, it might be an indicator that you have not yet forgiven them. If that's the case, you've got to stop here, and forgive anyone who holds the keys to your healing.

So, let's charge forward and deconstruct God's armor to understand exactly what it is. I've underlined points of emphasis so we can discuss.

> *Finally, my brethren, be strong in the Lord and in the power of His might.[11] Put on the <u>whole armor of God</u>, that ye may be able to <u>stand against the wiles of the devil</u>.[12] For we wrestle not <u>against flesh and blood</u>, but against principalities, against powers, against the <u>rulers of the darkness of this world</u>, against spiritual wickedness in high places.*
> *[13] Therefore, take unto you the whole armor of God, that ye may be able to withstand in the evil day and, having done all, to stand.[14] Stand*

therefore, having your <u>loins girded about with truth</u>, and having on the <u>breastplate of righteousness</u>, [15] and <u>your feet shod with the preparation of the Gospel of peace</u>.
[16] Above all, take the <u>shield of faith</u>, wherewith ye shall be able to quench all the fiery darts of the wicked. [17] And take the <u>helmet of salvation</u> and the <u>sword of the Spirit</u>, which is the Word of God,
[18] praying always with all prayer and supplication in the Spirit, and watching thereunto with all perseverance and supplication for all saints.
Ephesians 6:10-18

Important points:

1. Our fight is with the devil.
2. The devil's weapon is deception. Girding your loins (belt) of truth defeats lies and suspicions.
3. Breastplate of Righteousness defends our most vital organs, and defeats Satan's deadly tactic of casting shame and condemnation.
4. Our feet shod are the spikes roman soldiers wore to improve their stable footing in battle. Shod in peace is to have harmony with God.
5. Shield of Faith protects us from the fiery darts launched by the devil. His darts are pain, shame, and defeat.
6. Helmet of Salvation protects your other vital organ: your brain. Thought-life is where Satan finds the cracks to tempt you or deceive you through division. The helmet guards your thought-life.
7. Sword of the Spirit is God's word. This is your offensive weapon so that once the devil comes at you, like he did Jesus in the wilderness, you will repel him with God's truths.

Prayer is an important fortress, and it is also the direct line of communications with our four-star general in the times of warfare. God is our hope and our salvation. Remaining in close contact with Him during the battle will ensure victory over the enemy.

Praise and worship are another tool in our arsenal for repelling the devil's advances. Satan hates worship and praise. I mean he really hates it. The disciples Paul and Silas were locked up with no hope for release. Acts 16:25 tells of the ground erupting and the prison doors shaken open while they sang out praise from the deepest pit of the prison.

King David, who had faced so many dilemmas, also praised and worshipped God with his every fiber of being. He was delivered from the hands of death on several occasions during his times of offering praise in his pain (*Psalm 142:4-7*).

The last weapon for your spiritual fortress is to persevere. Victory in battle is seldom swift, and while the initial blows may seem to dictate a conqueror, perseverance is the key. Do you know how long the Hundred Year War lasted? Actually it's not a trick question, but it lasted 116 years. War is not only hell, but it can be long lasting.

We can look at Job for an example of persevering through pain. He'd lost everything except his faith in God. Like us, it may seem the hurting will never stop, but God has never once forsaken us or forgotten us. As we've been talking about, our healing is a process, and like Job, there is an end to the fighting and a blessing awaits.

Our past pain has been attached to us because we've not yet worked through the process. There is nothing that God cannot heal. And by heal, I mean, either by miraculous intervention, or over a period of time as you draw closer to Him.

God touched my heart years ago when I saw the story of Eva Moses Kor, a Holocaust survivor. She and her twin sister were subjected to horrific human experimentation under the direction of Josef Mengele at the Auschwitz concentration camp in Germany during World War II.

Although she lost both parents and two older sisters, she and her twin miraculously survived the torture and medical experiments. In 2015, she travelled back to Germany to testify at the trial of one of the doctors responsible for her and her sister's horror. She personally forgave him and the Nazis for what was done to her.

Heroes, this is perseverance!

If we armor up, pray, praise, and persevere, we will be delivered from the attacks that have stopped us from seeking healing for our past pain.

Submit yourselves, then, to God. Resist the devil, and he will flee from you.
James 4:7

Call To Action

1. Write out in detail what your spiritual armor looks like in a natural sense.
2. Write out a situation where you thought hope was lost, but you continued to praise God for every little step until you'd come through it.
3. Write out in detail an experience where God's healing or grace took longer than you had hoped, but when you had been delivered, what lesson was learned.

28

THE KEY TO FREEDOM

And you will know the truth, and the truth will set you free.
John 8:32

* * *

My brothers and sisters, this is always the hardest part to pen. There is so much that goes into writing these books, that instead of the end being the end, it is actually a new beginning. I learn so much during the research and am overwhelmed through prayers and memories of my own struggles.

Despite the temptation to dwell on my past of struggling with intimacy, addiction, and a distorted self-image, I've been set free thanks to a complete surrender to Christ. And to be completely open with you, the past pain still dredges up dark memories, but they no longer have authority over my life.

I don't think you ever "get over it," by pushing it to the back of your mind, or simply forgetting about it. Your past is a part of who you were, are, and will be. Like an injury scar to the body, it'll fade, but the cause of the scar no longer is the emergency it once was when you needed medical attention.

So as I wrote each section, some days took longer because the memories and emotions became too strong to keep writing through. That didn't mean I wasn't healed, it just meant I was human and no longer had to hide the way I felt about what had happened. Remember, our past is only to remind us, not to define us.

This is the point I pray you're at or soon will reach. Healing is a process, and the length of the process is up to you. I recall as my wife and I sat in a Christian marriage counselor's office, I asked him how long the process would take. He said the average was about five years. I laughed and said, "I'll beat that." The reality is, it'll take as long as the effort you are willing to put into it.

This book is so personal to me that I truly am thankful you've allowed me to work with you in your commitment to gain freedom from your past of personal pain. It not just changed but saved my life. I want you to be where I am too. There is nothing like the taste of freedom.

So many loved ones, friends, and acquaintances are pulling for you. The new you will also see how many other opportunities for getting back into a healthy, intentional life are waiting down the line. And you'll be a much better cop because of it.

This is a tough reality to face, so I pray you know what you've just accomplished. It's not easy to look at ourselves without blinking or making excuses for the bad behavior we've engaged in because of what someone or something did to us in our past. I've said it earlier, but while you are not responsible for what was done to you in your past, you are responsible for how you respond to it now.

Powering through this topic, while looking at yourself and the circumstances of your life, is taking that responsibility for it now. You've made a statement to you, and most importantly to God, that you will pursue and cling to Him for your freedom. No one I know has been freed and stayed free without Jesus Christ as the lead in their life. Stick to the Rock.

And, speaking of the Rock, I want to share my blessing with you. Jesus Christ has been so good to me but keeping the oil in my jar isn't fulfilling His calling to anoint other first responder heroes with God's healing grace. I prayed over every section before I began to write, and I'll continue to pray for everyone who has accepted and completed this challenge. There is healing to be gained, my friends.

God transcends what we understand as chronological time. He moves back and forth and side to side within our continuum. God has placed your blessing at a certain point in time, and it is waiting for you to continue pressing forward to claim it. That gift is freedom from all that haunts you. That freedom will bless you with a realistic view of your past life, and an optimistic view of your future.

I'm so fired up about what your future holds in store.

Rak Chazak Amats!!!

This is my prayer for you. The ancient Hebrew war cry encouraged God's warriors on to victory. It loosely means to be strong and of good courage, and to go forth without ever even considering the possibility of defeat.

Can you imagine living life with this stamped on our hearts? No enemy too big, too strong, too intimidating. No calling of God too big, too bold, too demanding.

Joshua 1 tells about God's command to Joshua just before he leads the nation into the promised land. There were still enemies trying to occupy what God had promised, but He assured Joshua of his success and inspired him to not be afraid, or discouraged, but rather be strong and courageous because God was with him.

Broken and Blue

"Have I not commanded you? Be strong and courageous. Do not be afraid; do not be discouraged, for the Lord your God will be with you wherever you go."
Joshua 1:9

God is with you, and your promised land is a life free from a painful past, and a future blessing of basking within the light of God's will. But first, you, just like I did, and Joshua did, must confront and slay your enemies who threaten to keep you away from God's promise.

Heroes, nothing you've been through or are going through is unknown to God. It's not ever too hard, too tough, or too deep for God to rescue you from it. But, like Jesus says in Revelation 3:20:

Here I am! I stand at the door and knock. If anyone hears my voice and opens the door, I will come in and eat with that person, and they with me.
Revelation 3:20

Knock, call, or cry out to Jesus, and He is there with you. No pride. No ego. No shame. Only Freedom. It is yours, warriors, if you're just willing to march forward with Rak Chazak Amats.

Here's to your freedom,
Scott

Call To Action

1. Write out in detail what it means to you to have finished this book.
2. Write out in detail what the next thirty days in your life will look like.

3. Write out in detail a letter to yourself telling you how proud you are for finishing this challenge.
4. Pat yourself on the back, and whisper;

"Rak Chazak Amats."
"Rak Chazak Amats."
"Rak Chazak Amats."

DR. SCOTT SILVERII

Dr. Scott Silverii is a son of the Living God. Thankful for the gift of his wife, Leah, they share seven kids, a French bulldog named Bacon and a micro-mini Goldendoodle named Biscuit.

A highly decorated, twenty-five-year law enforcement career promptly ended in retirement when God called Scott out of public service and into HIS service. The "Chief" admits that leading people to Christ is more exciting than the twelve years he spent undercover, sixteen years in SWAT, and five years as chief of police combined.

Scott has earned post-doctoral hours in a Doctor of Ministry degree in addition to a Master of Public Administration and a Ph.D. in Cultural Anthropology. Education and experience allow for a deeper understanding in ministering to the wounded, as he worked to break free from his own past pain and abuse.

In 2016, Scott was led to plant a church. Exclusive to online ministry, Five Stones Church.Online was born out of the calling to combat the negative influences reigning over social media. Scott's alpha manhood model for heroes is defined by, "Be on your guard; stand firm in the faith; be courageous; be strong. Do everything in love." (1 Corinthians 16:13-14)

YOUR MISSION ASSIGNMENT

Thanks again for your service.

Mission Checklist:

- Leave a review online wherever you bought this book. This really does help other 1st Responders find the help they need.

- Post the book and buy links on your social media so others find the help they need.

- Leave reviews anywhere that you may buy books and message boards.

- Message Chief Scott Silverii, PhD for interviews, speaking, blog tour or questions

ALSO BY CHIEF SCOTT SILVERII, PHD

Favored Not Forgotten: Embrace the Season, Thrive in Obscurity, Activate Your Purpose

Unbreakable: From Past Pain To Future Glory

Retrain Your Brain - Using Biblical Meditation To Purify Toxic Thoughts

God Made Man - Discovering Your Purpose and Living an Intentional Life

Captive No More - Freedom From Your Past of Pain, Shame and Guilt

Broken and Blue: A Policeman's Guide To Health, Hope, and Healing

Life After Divorce: Finding Light In Life's Darkest Season

Police Organization and Culture: Navigating Law Enforcement in Today's Hostile Environment

The ABCs of Marriage: Devotional and Coloring Book

Love's Letters (A Collection of Timeless Relationship Advice from Today's Hottest Marriage Experts)

A First Responder Devotional

40 Days to a Better Firefighter Marriage

40 Days to a Better Military Marriage

40 Days to a Better Corrections Officer Marriage

40 Days to a Better 911 Dispatcher Marriage

40 Days to a Better EMT Marriage

40 Days to a Better Police Marriage

More titles from Five Stones Press

fivestonespress.org

Made in the USA
Middletown, DE
29 June 2022